# MICKALENE THOMAS
# FEMMES NOIRES

Cover

**DIAHANN CARROLL #2 (DETAIL), 2017**

# MICKALENE THOMAS FEMMES NOIRES

EDITED BY ANDREA ANDERSSON & JULIE CROOKS

PUBLISHED BY

AGO

GOOSE LANE

IN ASSOCIATION WITH

Contemporary Arts Center New Orleans

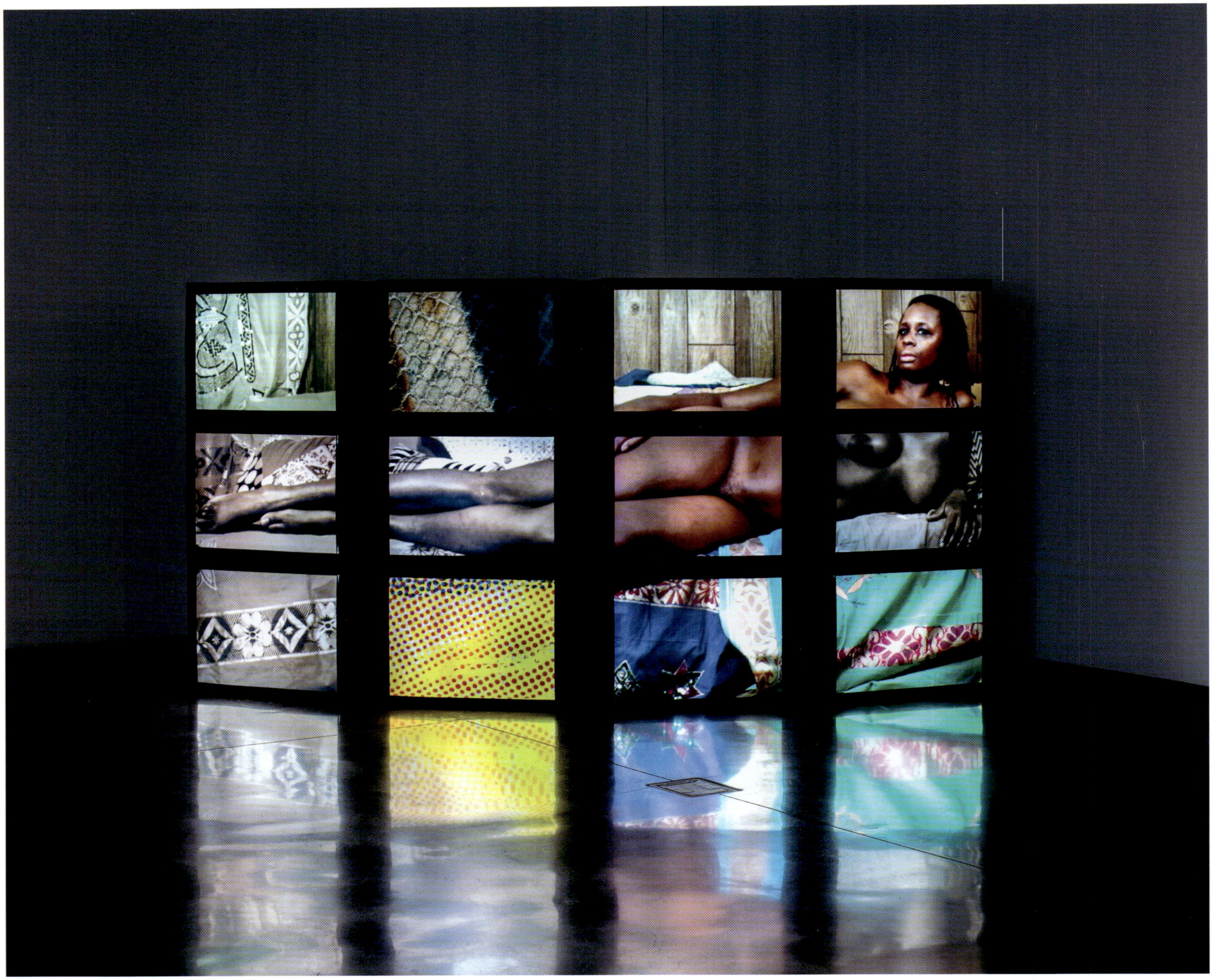

ME AS MUSE, 2016

**CONTENTS**

A major solo exhibition of work by the New York–based African-American artist Mickalene Thomas, *Femmes Noires* represents a partnership between the AGO and the Contemporary Arts Center, New Orleans—and an endeavour that feels especially timely. As a queer Black female artist, Thomas has gravitated toward collage, a medium that gives her free rein to play with multiple, intersecting points of view related to race, gender, and sexuality. *Mickalene Thomas: Femmes Noires* is a meditation on the politics of resistance. The focus is on Thomas's exuberant collage paintings, time-based media, silkscreened works, and photographs, featuring portraits of Black women—the *femmes noires* celebrated in the show's title. Our audiences will also have the opportunity to experience Thomas's elaborate living-room tableaux—sites that allow viewers to engage with this work in participatory, interactive, and multi-sensory ways.

In her work, Thomas seamlessly merges her biography with broader contemporary concerns around the cultural representation of Black women, at the same time drawing on and destabilizing the high modernist canon in Western art history. Her work is multidimensional, exploring cross-cultural, creolized, and hybridized notions of Black women's histories and their self-fashioning. As well, *Mickalene Thomas: Femmes Noires* is a collaboration realized through partners in Toronto and New Orleans, bridging divides between national borders and between the north and the south. It brings together communities, places, and histories, provoking necessary and often difficult conversations.

An exhibition such as this one requires an exceptional team of people with remarkable expertise and vision. I want to acknowledge the work of staff across the AGO in realizing this exhibition, particularly that of Julie Crooks, the AGO's Assistant Curator of Photography, project manager Valentine Moreno, interpretive planner Shiralee Hudson Hill, exhibition designer Flavio Trevisan, and curatorial administrative assistant Jill Offenbeck. I would also like to recognize the invaluable contributions of our partners at the Contemporary Arts Center in New Orleans, especially those of The Helis Foundation Chief Curator Andrea Andersson. As well, the Contemporary Arts Center extends its gratitude to The Helis Foundation as the Presenting Sponsor in New Orleans.

Thanks to Manager of Publishing Jim Shedden and the AGO's publishing department, especially Robyn Lew and Sarah Liss, as well as designer Lauren Wickware, for their work in producing this catalogue. Many thanks are also due to Antwaun Sargent and Carla Williams for their illuminating additions, and to the authors who gave their permission to publish the collage of fictional and scholarly excerpts that mirror many of the themes explored in this survey of work.

I thank the institutions, gallerists, and individual collectors who loaned works to the show: Jeff Vreeland at the Mickalene Thomas Studio, the National Gallery of Canada, the Montreal Museum of Fine Art, the Westmoreland Museum of American Art, Jean-Pierre and Rachel Lehmann, Anna Stothart at Lehmann Maupin Gallery, Galerie Nathalie Obadia, Mary Boone Gallery, Michael Bertrand, Maxine Granovsky Gluskin, George Hartman and Arlene Goldman, Ursula Burns, Haralambos (Harry) G. David, and Roberta and Michael Joseph.

We extend sincere gratitude to our valued supporters, whose philanthropy and enthusiasm for the exhibition have been inspiring. In particular, we appreciate the contributions of Lead Sponsor CIBC, and Lead Supporters Maxine Granovsky Gluskin & Ira Gluskin and Liza Mauer & Andrew Sheiner. Thanks also to Partners in Art and The Schulich Foundation for their generous support.

Finally, we extend profound thanks to Mickalene Thomas, whose virtuosic work demands that we re-examine and expand on the ways that transnational Black women are represented, viewed, and celebrated, not only in galleries, but across cultures.

Stephan Jost
Michael and Sonja Koerner Director, and CEO

# *Untitled: By Way of Introduction…*

## Andrea Andersson

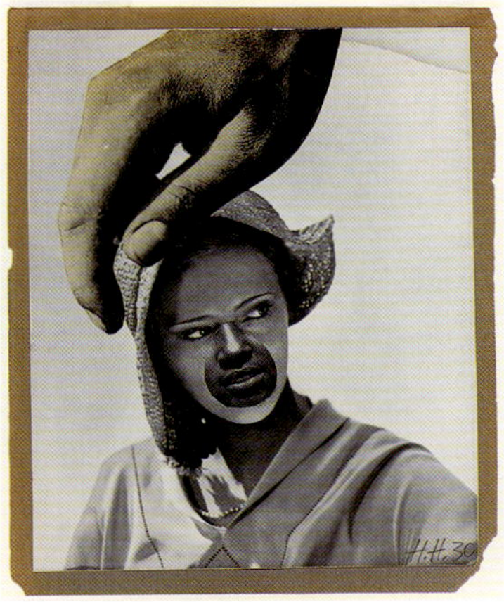

Hannah Höch, *Untitled (Large Hand Over Woman's Head)*, 1930. Photomontage, 25.7 × 20.7 cm.

Art Gallery of Ontario, purchase, 2012. 2012/5. © Estate of Hannah Höch/SOCAN (2018).

The work is commonly identified by its parenthetical title, which reads like a Vermeer, suggesting something both particular and pedestrian about its subject. She stares with confidence, almost indifference, at the large hand that stretches across and touches her forehead. The brown of the hand, lighter than the brown of her face, cut and pasted from another photograph. The geometry of a woman, composed of arranged shapes, like the geometry of a landscape. The superimposition of cut and disproportionate parts lays bare her composite identity, drawn from heterogeneous histories that would otherwise hide beneath her skin.

*Untitled (Large Hand Over Woman's Head)* (1930) is a photomontage by Hannah Höch in the collection of the Art Gallery of Ontario in Toronto. It dates to the years during which Höch worked on her photomontage series "From an Ethnographic Museum" (c. 1924–1934), in which she combined images of ethnographic objects, archived and categorized, with those of contemporary women. The "New Woman"—an ambiguous term coined during the years of the Weimar Republic—points to a host of competing, unfixed, and irreconcilable constructions of feminine identity during a time of socio-political rupture. So do Höch's portraits, born of fierce juxtaposition.

Mickalene Thomas has referenced Höch's work as a "historical thread"—a thread in a practice that self-consciously weaves art histories, canonical works by Manet, Courbet, Picasso, Duchamp, and Bearden. As a woman, Höch stands out on the list. Nevertheless, she stands alongside a host of fellow travellers with a commitment to collage and montage.

Layered in both materials and meanings, the montage affords multiple signification, allegorical extension. It is not prescriptive, but expansive; it absorbs not only all the histories of its combinatory elements, but all the associations living in the mind and experience of its viewer. It calls to many, but sustains various and competing messages.

Höch's work in the AGO's collection might be read as critique of a colonial and racist society. Perhaps the large hand is a sign of a hovering patriarchy—or perhaps it is meant to forge connection. In the work of Mickalene Thomas, I am invariably drawn to the hands—where they rest; what they touch, control, or support; to whom they belong; and whom they connect. In her work, Thomas constructs her own community, builds it up through arrangement from disparate corners, makes visible the strength inherent in connection. *Mickalene Thomas: Femmes Noires* is an exhibition as much about the primacy of collage and montage in Thomas's work as it is about her demonstration of radical connectivity among parts and people.

In the earliest conversations about a presenting partnership between the AGO and the Contemporary Arts Center, New Orleans, we imagined the communities brought into dialogue through this exhibition. We imagined women of the African diaspora, the "femmes noires" to whom Thomas has dedicated her practice, who, like the artist, resist monolithic portraits. This is an exhibition of Mickalene Thomas's New Women, living in countries across the globe, whose histories and identities are multiple, complex, and changing.

Andrea Andersson (BA, Stanford University; PhD, Columbia University) is The Helis Foundation Chief Curator of the Visual Arts at the Contemporary Arts Center, New Orleans. Her scholarship traces the legacy of the interdisciplinary avant-garde in contemporary art practice, with particular interest in its manifestations in today's Global South.

# *Mickalene Thomas: Femmes Noires*

Julie Crooks

Far from being eternally fixed in some essentialized past...which is waiting to be found and which when found will secure ourselves into eternity, identities are the names we give to the different ways we are positioned by, and position ourselves within the narratives of the past.[1]
—Stuart Hall, "Cultural Identity and Diaspora"

Not only will I look, I want my stare to change reality.[2]
—bell hooks, "The Oppositional Gaze"

To do the work that I do, I am asking of and looking to my sisters of the world.[3]
—Mickalene Thomas

Mickalene Thomas puts Black women at the centre of her practice. Her aim is to "present beauty and the Black body," she says: "You'll see me, therefore I exist."[4] Certainly, it is impossible to easily ignore or dismiss the (often larger-than-life) Black women one confronts upon encountering Thomas's work. Take, for example, the subject of *Shinique: Now I Know* (page 41). Here, Shinique—a name that resonates throughout the African diaspora, from Jamaica in Queens, New York, to Kingston, Jamaica[5]—reclines in the fashion of an Orientalist odalisque among a riotous mixture of printed cushions and textiles inspired by both Western and African patterns. Though her pose is relaxed, her direct stare oozes confidence and composure. But there's a lot more going on in this saturated mise-en-scene than just a powerful protagonist. The notion of the "strong" Black woman is itself a burden, one that demands an immovable stoicism from those very Black women it aims to elevate. Thomas skilfully navigates this conundrum by using the intimate and, at times, enigmatic confines of her portraiture to evoke both self-assurance and vulnerability in famous and not-so-famous subjects alike. "I think that with great strength, you understand your own vulnerability," Thomas notes. "Vulnerability is not about weakness; it's a softness, an awareness of yourself. I think you need to recognize vulnerability and power equally."[6]

Vulnerability is also inherent in her use of collage. For Thomas, collage speaks to the fragmentation of diasporic identities and the current of appropriation that vibrates around us at a constant hum. "Our culture is becoming so amalgamated," she said in an interview with art historian and professor Sarah Lewis in 2012. "Everyone's taking something on, appropriating...whose language is whose? That's how I see collage, it's really wanting to play with these kinds of images and patterns and ask where did they come from and how were they incorporated and constructed?"[7] Her artistic process is multistep and multimedia, lending itself to the mutability of collage. For Thomas, this technique registers Black womanhood and subjectivity in the histories of art and popular culture. Her project presents a plethora of references, negotiations, and aesthetic choices which, when brought together (or collaged), create new possibilities for seeing a range of beautiful Black bodies.

Those bodies are central and celebrated in *Mickalene Thomas: Femmes Noires*, Thomas's first solo Canadian show, presented by the AGO in partnership with the Contemporary Arts Center, New Orleans. The exhibition is grounded in the use of collage, which critic Lucy Lippard has described as "an aesthetic that willfully takes apart what is or is supposed to be and rearranges it in ways that suggest what it could be."[8] *Mickalene Thomas: Femmes Noires* firmly locates Thomas's interest in the politicized potential of collage as a strategy to amalgamate the disparate pieces of lived (often precarious) experience that together constitute a fragmented whole: a Black diasporic sisterhood! (In keeping with the themes of collaged interventions, this catalogue also includes essays and excerpts by leading fiction writers, artists, and essayists that help to contextualize the importance of Thomas's work from multiple gendered and Black diasporic perspectives.)

The exhibition mimics the formal nature of collage, suturing together Thomas's multimedia paintings, photographs, videos, and immersive tableaux in the gallery space. In dialogue with the collages of Romare Bearden, Lubaina Himid, Wangechi Mutu, and Black Canadian artists Bushra Junaid and June Clark, *Mickalene Thomas: Femmes Noires* creates a space where Black female subjects are hyper-visible and omnipresent. Frequently larger than life, Thomas's subjects stare back and down at the viewer—a transformative example of the "oppositional gaze"[9] mentioned by hooks in the epigraph.

As well, this show plays on interventionist strategies linked to contemporary Black popular culture and art histories. One such intervention occurred recently when Beyoncé Knowles-Carter took over the Louvre with her husband, Jay-Z. In their music video for "Apeshit" (2018), the couple and dozens of dancers deftly address the historical erasure of Black representation in a space seen as a bastion of European art. Though these interventions have come to be regarded as radical

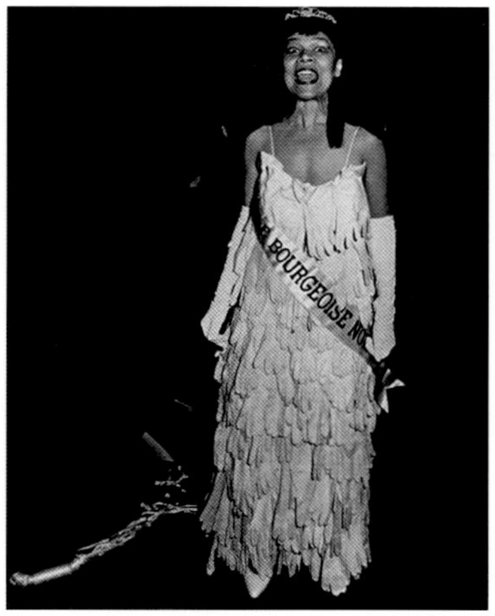

Lorraine O'Grady, *Untitled (Mlle Bourgeoise Noire Shouts Out Her Poem)*, 1980–1983/2009. Silver gelatin print, 24.61 × 19.05 cm.



and transformative by and for the millennial generation, they've been par for the course for Black women artists such as Betye Saar, Faith Ringgold, and Lorraine O'Grady (to name just a few) since the 1980s. In 1980, O'Grady famously donned a white gown constructed of white gloves, along with a crown and sash, to become her alter ego, *Mademoiselle Bourgeoisie Noire* ("Miss Black Middle Class"). She would show up at mainstream art galleries and flagellate herself with a cat-o'-nine-tails while challenging her audience with proclamations ("Black art must take more risks!" and "Now is the time for an invasion!"[10]), calling attention to the plight of Black artists erased from the mainstream art world.

While the material realities and injustices related to race, gender, and sexuality persist, *Mickalene Thomas: Femmes Noires* presents an overt opportunity to make an intervention in a traditionally white space which has historically excluded marginalized and racialized artists.

**BEGINNINGS: THE CUT 'N' MIX**

Mickalene Thomas was born in 1971 in Camden, New Jersey, and came of age in the 1970s, a volatile period at the end of the civil rights era. At the time, Black nationalism and the "Black Is Beautiful" movement were on the rise, both of which challenged and transformed common Western notions of beauty in the United States and across the Black Atlantic world (including Canada). Reinvigorated conversations about the possibilities of Pan-Africanism, both on the African continent and in parts of the Caribbean, added to this ferment.

The 1970s also saw the rise of Black cultural icons: Black action cinema showcased fierce stars such as Pam Grier; popular music celebrated Black divas such as Diana Ross, Diahann Carroll, and Eartha Kitt; and the fashion world made space for model Naomi Sims. Meanwhile, powerful figures such as Nina Simone, Angela Davis, and Kathleen Cleaver were held up as both activists and trendsetters. However, I would argue that the movement which left the most indelible mark on Thomas's consciousness—and, by extension, her art practice—was second-wave feminism and, crucially, the important responses of Black women to its proposals. Many felt "mainstream" feminism omitted vital issues around race, class, and sexuality that deeply affected the lives of Black women globally.[11] The notion of intersectionality[12] was the founding principle of the Combahee River Collective, a Black lesbian activist organization that came up with the (now frequently misused) phrase "identity politics."[13] As Thomas recalls, "The 1970s were a tumultuous time for many people…here were many, mostly marginalized, communities mobilizing to create liberated spaces for themselves. All of these black, queer, women-centered communities protested against conservatism and the oppressive nature of tradition. And amidst all of this upheaval, great music, fashion, and art were created."[14]

That era provided the conceptual backdrop to Thomas's work, but her practice was also influenced by formal training. In 2000, Thomas graduated from the Pratt Institute, where she completed her BFA with a concentration on painting; she earned her MFA from Yale University in 2002. From the onset, Thomas was interested in work that depicted Black womanhood. She was determined to reflect the lived experiences of herself and her peers, always with the aim of claiming subjectivity in the face of daily structural violence. Her multidimensional practice has created space for the cut 'n' mix[15]—a term originating in popular music, used to describe the editing process—evident in her exquisite paintings, photography, innovative videos, and living-room tableaux.

Although Thomas's consciousness has clearly been influenced by the feminist and Black Power movements of her formative years, her own Black aesthetic is also anchored in references both communal—music of the era, such as disco, funk, soul, R&B, and hip-hop; cultural staples such as *Soul Train*; and Black-focused beauty and lifestyle magazines such as *Essence* and *Ebony*—and personal. Alongside models, she often uses a diverse range of friends, former lovers, and her partner, Racquel Chevremont, who become the empowered muses in her intimately rendered portraits. And the sensibility behind those portraits was shaped by a genealogy of Black women, including her grandmother and her mother, Sandra Bush. Thomas has reflected on how these influences have shaped her work: "When I started making the paintings and the installations, I started thinking about how my grandmother used different materials to reupholster her furniture…or patch it up. I was taking elements that I remembered as very powerful, like the Afro, the faux paneling, the patterns that I was surrounded by, and putting that into my work."[16]

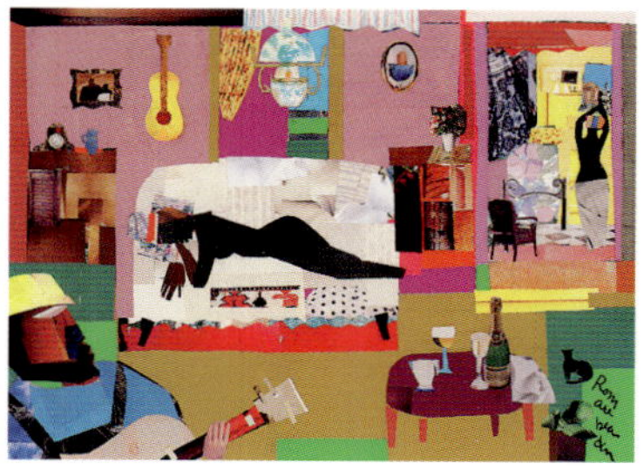

Romare Bearden, *Black Venus*, 1968.
Mixed-media collage, 75.56 × 102.07 cm.

Mildred Lane Kemper Art Museum, Washington University in St. Louis. University purchase, Charles H. Yalem Art Fund, 1994. 

## THE POETICS OF COLLAGE

Thomas's highly expressive images appropriate and recontextualize iconic works in the Western art canon. As such, her deployment of collage (the word is rooted in the French *coller*, meaning "to paste, stick or glue"), a technique that the American art historian and essayist Clement Greenberg describes as "a major turning point in the whole evolution of modernist art,"[17] is wilful, executed with an eye to her artistic predecessors while maintaining her footing in the contemporary present. Early avant-garde artists, most notably Pablo Picasso and Georges Braque, explored the liberatory possibilities of this form. The very material and technical nature of collage-making allowed for infinite ways in which to deconstruct, cut, appropriate, fragment, and repurpose myriad elements to form both new pictorial contexts and collapse senses of time and space. As Katherine Hoffman notes, "Collage introduced an interaction between the pictorial surface and the real environment...freeing the artist from the technicalities of brushwork."[18] Collage was augmented in the early twentieth century by the Surrealists, who infused it with dreamlike qualities, and Dadaists such as Hannah Höch, who expanded the technique with the addition of photographic images and acerbic social commentary.

While collage was born out of the European avant-garde, critics have argued that (similar to much of the Cubist movement) these forms were informed by a hybridized multiracial and transatlantic world.[19] Hoffman is more specific, suggesting that "Picasso was likely influenced by the assembled and synthetic qualities of African objects that used materials such as beads, shells and fabric."[20] It is perhaps not surprising, then, that collage-like practices were deployed by a variety of Black artists during the Harlem Renaissance as a tool to express the hybridity of African-American vernacular forms and modernism. One of the most notable exemplars of this practice was Romare Bearden (1911–1988), who switched from painting to collage-making in the 1960s. Bearden viewed this method as a way to grapple with representing Black bodies outside of popular romantic notions of Africa and essentialized conceptions of the homogeneity of African-American identities.[21] He noted, "I felt that the Negro was becoming too much of an abstraction, rather than the reality that art can give a subject."[22] By the mid-1960s, he was drawing on recurring motifs: blues guitarists, mothers and children, women in interior spaces, scenes evoking urban America. Sourcing photographs from a variety of magazines and archives, Bearden created collages with images that depicted a wide range of Black experiences in the diaspora. In doing so, he merged the complexities of both high modernism and the Black vernacular.[23]

Writer Ralph Ellison suggests that through the fragmentary nature of collage, Bearden's work made "the unseen manifest."[24] This is deftly illustrated in the artist's *Black Venus*, from 1968. Here, Bearden uses the language of modernism and Orientalism, situating the figure of a Black female odalisque at the centre of the composition. Bearden may have been cheekily responding to Manet's *Olympia* (1863) by erasing altogether the figure of Victorine Meurent, the white model central to the painting, instead making the Black maid, Laure, manifest, taking up a primary place in the work. The assembling of the disparate elements which constitute *Black Venus* is emblematic of the multidimensionality of Black identities and subjectivities evoked in Bearden's collages.

### A HISTORY OF *FEMMES NOIRES*

The visible racialized threads in Thomas's work engage the roots of collage, tracing a diffuse lineage that includes Wangechi Mutu, Kara Walker, and the more recent work of Deborah Roberts, among others—all Black female artists who expand on Bearden's hybridized methodologies through their own gendered collage practices. This lineage is also useful for understanding the underlying meanings and manifestations of collage in Mickalene Thomas's practice and in the context of *Femmes Noires*.

Like Bearden, who stated, "I paint on collage. I consider them paintings,"[25] Thomas views herself as a painter. The style, composition, and heroic scale of her work mirror the compositions and tropes of the so-called European Old Masters. Yet Thomas's mastery is in the ways in which self-possessed Black women sit, lounge, or stand at the focal point of each of her paintings. Kerry James Marshall has underscored the importance of context in Thomas's works and refers to such context as a "Black aesthetic,"[26] which he describes as "works that draw upon, allude to, and riff on the sensibility and material production of various 'Black diasporic' clusters. Black aesthetics is an atmosphere, a tone, a vibe." A Black aesthetic is "glamorous and impoverished, structured and improvisational, naive and sophisticated, brash and abject. Its first principle is a desire for self-representation."[27] This notion is at the heart of the works presented in *Femmes Noires*.

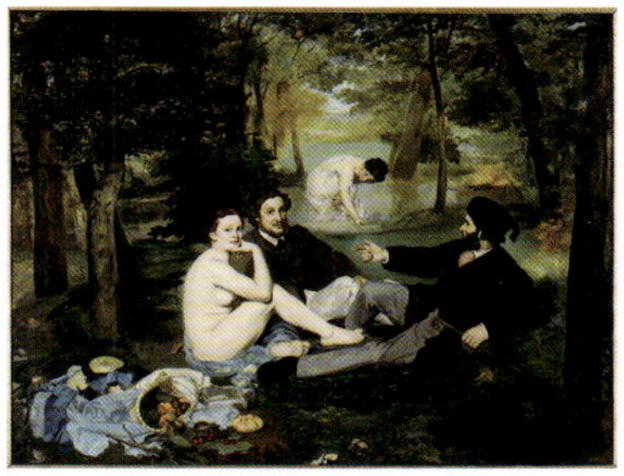

Édouard Manet, *Le déjeuner sur l'herbe*, 1863. Oil on canvas, 208 × 264.5 cm.
Musée d'Orsay, Paris, France. RF1668.

To produce her paintings, Thomas first photographs her subjects in staged environments in her studio—redolent of the 1970s, these constructed sets replicate living-room interiors outfitted with faux-wood panels. Her compositions pop with an assortment of densely patterned fabrics, both on furniture and worn by the subject, as well as other stylized and decorative accoutrements; the vibrant sets reference the work of modernist Malian photographer Malick Sidibé, among others. In these close interior spaces, Africa and the diaspora co-mingle. After creating the initial image, Thomas creates a smaller-scale collage by cutting, sourcing, and reassembling parts of the photograph, creating a flattened surface and a diminished depth. Lastly, Thomas paints a large-scale version—and adds embellishments, such as her signature Swarovski rhinestones.

This idiosyncratic process results in work like *I Learned the Hard Way* (2010) (page 75). The monumental painting, which uses acrylic, enamel, and rhinestones on a wood panel, takes its name from a song by the late Sharon Jones[28] and her band, the Dap-Kings. Jones sung the tune—which tells the story of a woman duped by an unfaithful lover—with soulful resignation, and with the groovy assurance that the truth was liberating. In Thomas's piece, the subject sits with her legs demurely crossed at the knees, one foot slightly in front of the other. She sits ramrod straight in the centre, with a fabulous golden Afro (made even more luminous by the embedded gold rhinestones) forming a triumphant apex. One is struck by the palpable sense of control, and the unwavering intensity of her gaze! Describing Thomas's paintings, Derek Conrad Murray observes that "the black-female body is often alone, isolated, a sight of viewing pleasure, but also impudent and disobedient."[29] The collaged patterns create a patchwork of jagged shapes in varied sizes and explosions of colour, forming a flattened, layered space upon which Thomas situates her imposing model.

Where *I Learned the Hard Way* riffs on contemporary popular Black culture, Thomas's iconoclastic masterpiece, *Le déjeuner sur l'herbe: Les trois femmes noires* (2010) (pages 50–51) is an intentional interrogation and undoing of high modernism. The painting is massive, measuring more than seven metres in length. While Thomas's reimagining openly gestures to Édouard Manet's *Le déjeuner sur l'herbe* (1863), her centring of the *trois femmes noires* is a transgressive reimagination of the original. In Manet's painting, two prostitutes and two dandy-like gentlemen form the focus of the work. One of the women, who is nude, stares coolly back at the viewer. The painting, considered scandalous in its day, rendered classically posed subjects in a contemporary setting— a break from established conventions

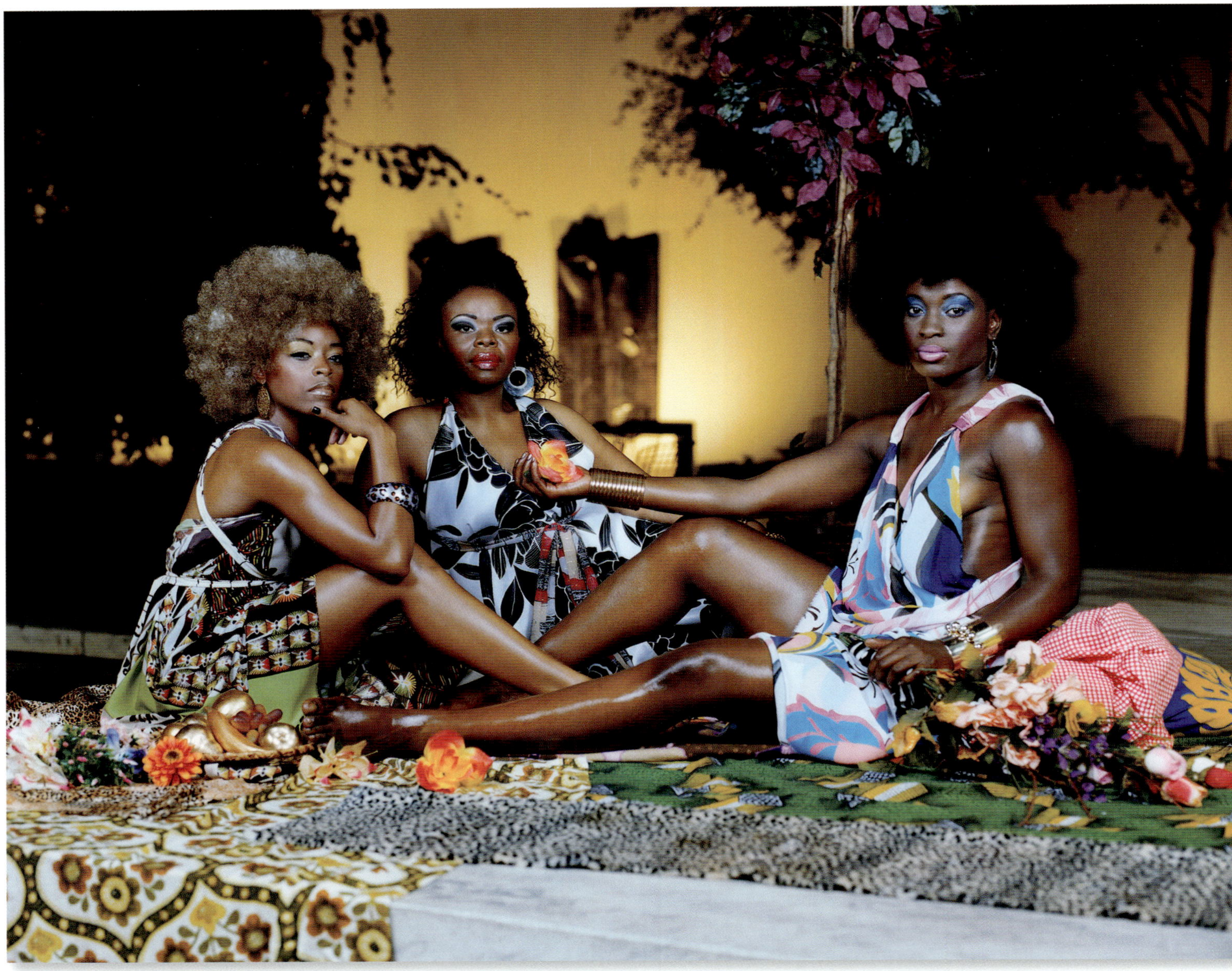

LE DÉJEUNER SUR L'HERBE: LES TROIS FEMMES NOIRES, 2010

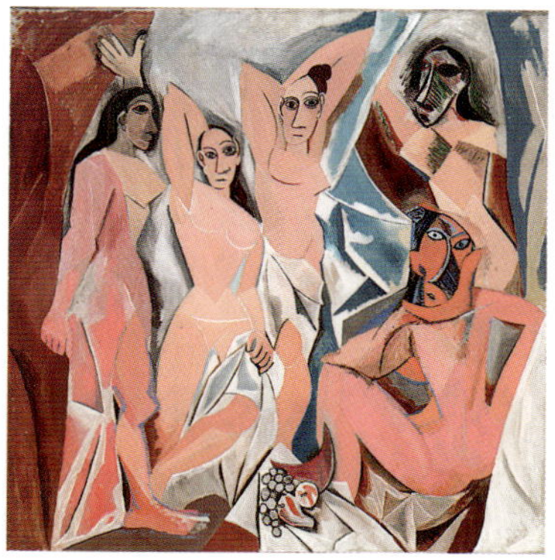

Pablo Picasso. *Les Demoiselles d'Avignon*, 1907. Oil on canvas, 243.9 × 233.7 cm.

The Museum of Modern Art, New York, acquired through the Lillie P. Bliss Bequest. © Picasso Estate / SOCAN (2018).

that was seen as a radical no-no at the time. It is not surprising that Thomas feels a "kinship and imperative"[30] with the father of modernism while at the same time confronting the movement's failures. Recalling Marshall's "diasporic clusters," the three fully clothed Black women at the centre of Thomas's *Le déjeuner sur l'herbe* are the direct descendants of modernity's economic dependence on the plunder of Africa in the form of European colonialism and the Transatlantic slave trade. The painting evokes the violence of such encounters and histories, while its jagged fragmented shapes and frenzied lines are also symbolic of Black women's continuing struggle for self-representation beyond static stereotypes.

*Le déjeuner sur l'herbe: Les trois femmes noires* began as a photograph (page 20) commissioned by MoMA and staged in the museum's sculpture garden. The photographed version has the appearance of a high-fashion magazine shoot, replete with glamorous Black models wearing over-the-top makeup and chic attire, set against the beautifully lit backdrop of the MoMA. In contrast, the painted version features a riot of fragments and fissures, with multiple patterns providing a contrast against the flat matte colouring of the women's skin tones, which range from caramel to dark chocolate. Here, Thomas's process highlights not only the materiality of the painting but also the fraught battles Black women fought and continue to fight against global systems of oppression. The three women depicted demand to be seen as subjects with agency. They are made "manifest" within the fragmented surface. Lippard is useful here in her assessment of collage as a possibility for radical feminist art practice. Collage, she writes, "is about shifting relationships, juxtaposition and superimposition, gluing and ungluing."[31] Thomas has destabilized the modernist past, and realized through her brilliant execution the post-postmodern future—Lippard's suggestion of *what could be*. Thomas is fearless in her interest in experimentation, in the limitless potential of her practice to represent Black women's futurity in the present.[32]

This conscious tension between the past and the future-present fuels Thomas's newer paintings. *Portrait of Kalena* (2017) (page 99), presents a more minimalist portrait in oil and acrylic paint, with a background set in muted tones. In contrast to Thomas's earlier paintings, the viewer does not have full access to the sitter, whose face is partially obscured by a mask. Here, the artist makes an explicit reference to Picasso that calls to mind the visages of the women depicted in the celebrated *Les Demoiselles d'Avignon* (1907). Thomas reappropriates the geometric shapes and masklike elements of the original. By wresting the mask-like figure from the clutches of high modernism and investing it with new meaning in a new context, Thomas underscores her deep understanding of the ways in which Black women's bodies have been hyper-racialized and hyper-surveilled.[33] Thomas is also interrogating how we view the Black female figure—and its erasure—in canonical art history. "The Western art-historical moments that I am extracting as a source for my practice are not about reclaiming," she has said; "it's about acknowledging that the space was always ours—about owning that space."[34] In other words, she offers up a vision of Black futurity.

#### I'M EVERY WOMAN

Although Thomas may be best known for large-scale collage paintings, she carries her core ideology into her work in other media. The layers and fragmentation so crucial to her collages are echoed in the "superimpositions and juxtapositions" prominently featured in the artist's time-based media and silkscreen mirrored works. For Thomas, the video format is integral to the development of her work in collage. "The editing process reminded me of collage. Once I started editing… I saw myself thinking about cutting paper and deconstructing the image with multiple layers."[35] These works use found footage to examine ideas around beauty, as well as the glare and instability of celebrity.

*Do I Look Like a Lady? (Comedians and Singers)*, from 2016 (pages 102–103), is a twelve-minute, two-channel video in which Thomas brings together found YouTube footage of a range of Black female performers (across time, geographical space, and genre) expressing their takes on femininity, respectability politics, and complex notions of Black beauty. Thomas separates the performers by genre: comedians occupy one screen, singers another. She manipulates the video material, creating a grid-like pattern of montages, with the two sets of women on screen engaged in an intersectional conversation. There is connective tissue that binds these collaged moving parts: as Thomas notes, "the sense of their lyrics and sound…together, the thread of the music and jokes tell a story of being a black woman."[36] Thomas underscores the importance of gaining control of the narrative voice for racialized women artists. As Nina Simone sings her medley "Ain't Got No/I Got Life," Whoopi Goldberg does her white-girl routine from *The Spook Show*, Josephine Baker performs her iconic shadow dance, and Whitney Houston begins belting out "The Greatest Love of All." As a young person, Thomas admired these performers, who were also admired by her mother and grandmother. They also held an important and pivotal place for a generation of Black women globally as their performances circulated beyond the United States in the international sphere. Now, through her artistic practice, Thomas has synthesized and transmuted the influences of her foremothers, as she herself becomes part of the next generation of female icons in the canon of art history.

Juxtaposed with these video installations, Thomas's silkscreened ink-mirror works continue her visual homage to and exploration of the multiplicities of Black female identities. Here, she adds portraits of women who have helped shape notions of the Black celebrity diva: beautiful, strong, and fragile (like the mirrored surfaces on which they are pictured) (pages 44, 98, 106, 108, 120). These large, irregularly shaped works feature the likenesses of Diahann Carroll, who in the 1960s challenged racial barriers in Hollywood by becoming the first Black woman to star in her own sitcom; Naomi Sims, the first Black "supermodel" (the concept had yet to be invented in the late 1960s); and Diana Ross, the lead singer of the Supremes and a Black celebrity icon in her own right. Each piece is constructed of fragments or shards of mirror that break up the picture plane. Creating the work is laborious but underscores the deep materiality of each work—a quality that is immensely important for Thomas. "Materiality is one of the most significant aspects of my practice," she has noted. "Beginning with the process of collage allows me to better translate those qualities when I create the larger works. I then utilize the different textures of rhinestones, glitter, oil, acrylic, silkscreen, and varnish to recreate the sense and feeling of a collage on canvas and to establish dynamic compositions that play with formal aspects of painting."[37] The ghostly holographic and painterly effects created by these reflective surfaces require that viewers spend time with the work in order to discern the multiple and varied perspectives—a "reflection," so to speak, of the myriad aspects of African diasporic womanhood. These mirrored works also reflect "racialized icons"[38] such as Ross, Sims, Carroll, and other pop-cultural change-makers as a way of acknowledging their importance within the panoply of Black women and global visibility.

Biography—a visualization of and participation in internal reflection—is also key to *Mickalene Thomas: Femmes Noires*, as evinced by the artist's immersive tableaux. These installations mimic domestic interior spaces, such as living or recreational rooms, which encourage the viewer to actively participate by sitting to view select videos (pages 109, 111). These environments, which include chairs, stools, ottomans, floor tiles, tables, and cushions in a range of colourful prints, fabrics, and styles, are based heavily on Thomas's recollections of childhood living rooms decorated by her mother and grandmother. "I imagine the spaces from earlier in my life: my grandmother's house, my aunt's house, my uncle's house, my mother's house," she has said. "My interiors partly reflect my nostalgia for how I lived."[39] These environments serve as diasporic spaces of comfort and intimacy—not only for Thomas, but for those of us who viscerally experience/d the recreation and living-room spaces of our childhood homes, spaces outfitted with wood-panelled walls, plastic-covered sofas (or settees, depending on your locale), chairs laden with cushions and throws, ottomans, retro lamps, tiles, and carpeting, fake flowers, and wood-encased radio/television set combos.[40] The hyper-dressed tableau is further contextualized with the addition of faux and live plants and stacks of books by influential Black writers from Africa and the diaspora: Chimamanda Ngozi Adichie, Alice Walker, Eldridge Cleaver, Jamaica Kincaid, Toni Morrison, Makeda Silvera, and many more. Audience members are encouraged to leaf through books of interest (and to borrow them, with the promise of returning), creating a haptic multi-sensory experience in the gallery. Here, Thomas creates a place of refuge for audiences to contemplate the capacious and comprehensive parts of her Black aesthetic enterprise.

*Mickalene Thomas: Femmes Noires* brings together the heterogeneous mediums, modalities, and forms of Thomas's collage practices, which she uses to upend monolithic notions and representations of Black women. Thomas is the second Black female artist to have a solo exhibition presented at the AGO—after Wangechi Mutu, whose 2010 exhibition, *This You Call Civilization*, showcased her own use of collage. It is worth noting that both artists draw on the same central aesthetic strategy. How are we to reflect on this, the use of collage by Black female artists as a tool of subversion, as an approach that lays bare gendered and racialized bodies in the mainstream gallery setting? The exhibition presented at the AGO and at the CAC in New Orleans is a celebration of Thomas's impressive artistic accomplishments to date. One hopes that it also opens up the possibilities for her work to inspire transnationally engaged dialogues concerning race, gender, class, and sexuality with those who envision Black futurity today.

Julie Crooks is the Assistant Curator of Photography at the Art Gallery of Ontario. She received her PhD from the Department of History of Art and Archaeology at the School of Oriental and African Studies (SOAS), University of London, where her research focused on historical photography in Sierra Leone, West Africa, and the diaspora. Prior to joining the AGO, she curated and co-curated a number of exhibitions in Toronto, including *No Justice, No Peace: From Ferguson to Toronto* in February 2017, co-curated with Reese de Guzman (co-organized by the Ryerson Image Centre and BAND).

**1** Stuart Hall, "Cultural Identity and Diaspora," in J. Rutherford, ed., *Identity: Culture, Community, Difference* (London: Lawrence and Wishart, 1990), 225.

**2** bell hooks, "The Oppositional Gaze," in *Black Looks: Race and Representation* (New York: South End Press, 1992), 116.

**3** Dr. Mia Bagneris, *Mickalene Thomas: Waiting on a Prime-Time Star* exhibition program (New Orleans: Newcomb Art Museum of Tulane, September 2016), 6.

**4** Matthew Tedford Harrison, "Mickalene Thomas," *ArtPractical*, Sept. 13, 2013, https://www.artpractical.com/column/mickalene-thomas/.

**5** Stephen Crockett, "LaKeisha, Where Art Thou? The Case for Black-Sounding Names," *The Root*, May 30, 2017, https://www.theroot.com/lakeisha-where-art-thou-the-case-for-black-sounding-1795642640.

**6** Bagneris, *Mickalene Thomas: Waiting on a Prime-Time Star*, 6.

**7** Sarah Lewis, "Mickalene Thomas on Beauty," in Lisa Melandri, ed., *Mickalene Thomas: Origin of the Universe* (Santa Monica: Santa Monica Museum of Art, 2012), 11.

**8** Lucy Lippard, "No Regrets," *Art in America*, no. 95 (June 2007): 75.

**9** hooks, *Black Looks: Race and Representation*, 116.

**10** Stephanie Sparling Williams, "Frame Me: Speaking Out of Turn and Lorraine O'Grady's Alien Avant Garde," *Stedelijk Studies* no. 3 (Fall 2015), https://stedelijkstudies.com/journal/frame-me-speaking-out-of-turn-and-lorraine-ogradys-alien-avant-garde/.

**11** See Benita Roth, "Second Wave Black Feminism in the African Diaspora: News from New Scholarship," *Agenda: Empowering Women for Gender Equity*, no. 58 (2003), 46–48.

**12** Intersectionality is a theory or framework for understanding the ways in which people are disenfranchised by a range of oppressions based on race, class, gender, and sexual orientation. See Kimberle Crenshaw, "Demarginalizing the Intersection of Race and Sex: A Black Feminist Critique of Antidiscrimination Doctrine, Feminist Theory and Antiracist Politics," *University of Chicago Legal Forum* (1989): 1.

**13** Mychal Denzel Smith, "What Liberals Got Wrong about Identity Politics," *The New Republic*, Sept. 11, 2017, https://newrepublic.com/article/144739/liberals-get-wrong-identity-politics.

**14** Miss Rosen, "Artist Mickalene Thomas Makes Portraits to Bring Out Your Inner Foxy Brown," *Dazed & Confused*, Apr. 5, 2018, http://www.dazeddigital.com/art-photography/article/39571/1/artist-mickalene-thomas-talks-painting-self-love-and-real-beautiful-women.

**15** Dick Hebdige, *Cut 'n' Mix: Culture, Identity and Caribbean Music* (London and New York: Comedia/Methuen, 1987), 10.

**16** Maja Horn, "The Multiple Media and Modes of Visibility of Mickalene Thomas," *ArtPulse*, Feb. 28, 2012, http://artpulse-magazine.com/the-multiple-media-and-modes-of-visibility-of-mickalene-thomas.

**17** Clement Greenberg, "Collage," in *Art and Culture: Critical Essays* (Boston: Beacon Press, 1961), 70.

**18** Katherine Hoffman, "Collage in the Twentieth Century: an Overview," in Katherine Hoffman, ed., *Collage: Critical Views* (Ann Arbor, MI: UMI Research Press, 1989), 6.

**19** Helen Carr, "Imagism and Empire," in Howard J. Booth and Nigel Rigby, eds., *Modernism and Empire* (Manchester: Manchester University Press, 2000), 87.

**20** Hoffman, *Collage: Critical Views*, 6.

**21** See Kobena Mercer, "Romare Bearden, 1964: Collage as Knothole," in *Cosmopolitan Modernisms* (Cambridge, MA: MIT Press, 2005), 125.

**22** Sharon Patton, *African American Art* (Oxford: Oxford University Press, 1998), 187.

**23** Mercer, *Cosmopolitan Modernisms*, 125.

**24** Ralph Ellison, "The Art of Romare Bearden," *Massachusetts Review* 18, no. 4 (1977), 679.

**25** Sharon F. Patton, *Memory and Metaphor: The Art of Romare Bearden, 1940–1987*, (New York: Studio Museum of Harlem, 1991), 48.

**26** Kerry James Marshall, "Mickalene's Harem," in *Kerry James Marshall: Mastry* (New York: Museum of Modern Art, 2016), 241.

**27** Ibid.

**28** Sharon Jones was a celebrated funk-soul singer who found success with her band the Dap-Kings. She died in 2016, at the age of 60.

**29** Derek Conrad Murray, "Loving Aberrance: Mickalene Thomas and the Queering of Black Female Desire," in *Queering Post-Black Art: Artists Transforming African-American Identity After Civil Rights* (London and New York: I.B. Taurus & Co. Ltd., 2016), 120.

**30** Matthew McLendon, "Interview with Mickalen Thomas," *Beyond the Bling: Voices of Hip Hop in Art* (Sarasota, Florida: John and Mable Ringling Museum of Art, Florida State University, 2011), 115.

**31** Lippard, "No Regrets."

**32** See Tina Campt, *Listening to Images* (Durham , NC: Duke University Press, 2017), 17, in which she argues for a Black feminist grammar of futurity to think through the notion of "a politics of prefiguration that involves living the present in the now—as striving for the future we want to see…in the present."

**33** The original models for Picasso's work may have been influenced by postcard images of African women by French photographer Edmond Fortier, who took pictures on the coast of French West Africa and was based in Dakar between 1900 and 1901. Picasso collected many of Fortier's postcards. See David Baldassari's *The Dark Mirror* (1998).

**34** Bagneris, *Mickalene Thomas: Waiting on a Prime-Time Star*, 4.

**35** Sara Roffino, "Artist Mickalene Thomas Opens up Her Home and Studio," *Cultured,* Sept. 2017, https://www.culturedmag.com/mickalene-thomas/.

**36** Antwaun Sargent, "Mickalene Thomas on Muses, Models and Mentors," *Interview*, March 9, 2016, https://www.interviewmagazine.com/art/mickalene-thomas.

**37** Andre Naquain Wheeler, "Mickalene Thomas's Bedazzled Paintings Empower Black Women," *i-D*, Apr. 12, 2018, https://i-d.vice.com/en_us/article/9kggv8/mickalene-thomass-bedazzled-paintings-empower-black-women/.

**38** See Nicole R. Fleetwood, *On Racial Icons: Blackness and the Public Imagination* (Princeton, NJ: Rutgers University Press, 2015).

**39** Nicholas Boston, "Female Genius Mickalene Thomas," *Topical Cream*, Jan. 22, 2016, http://topicalcream.info/editorial/female-genius-mickalene-thomas.

**40** See Michael McMillan, "The 'West Indian' Front Room: Reflections on a Diasporic Phenomenon," *Kunapipi* 30, no. 2, 2008.

*Mickalene Thomas: Femmes Noires* references various texts from literature, history, art history, and popular culture. To amplify Thomas's use of collage as a structuring device and guiding philosophy, this catalogue includes a number of previously published critical essays and literary excerpts by Black female authors, presented in concert with the artist's own work. The varied voices of these writers call forth a range of identities, experiences, and narratives of women in the global African diaspora.

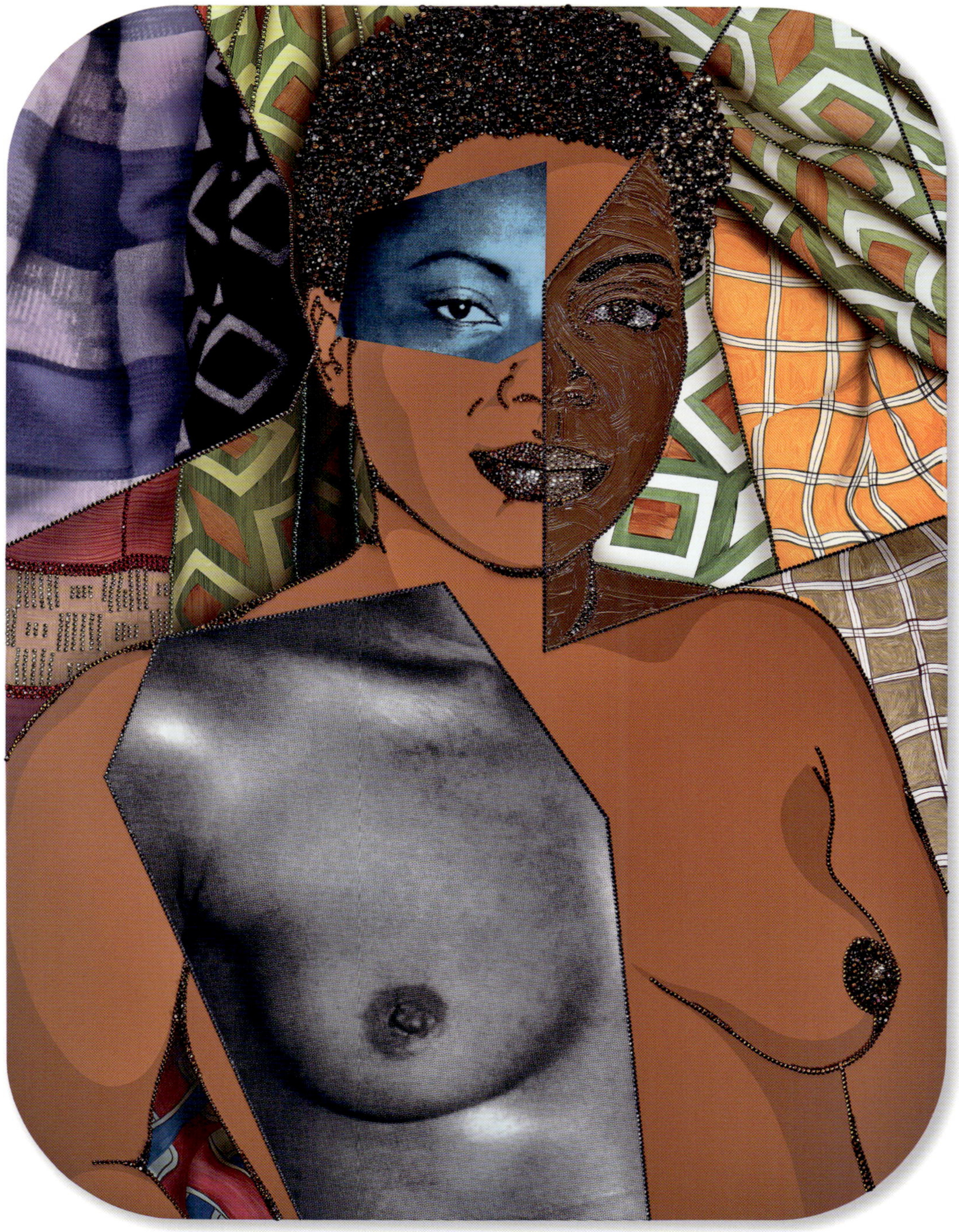

PORTRAIT OF MARIE, 2015

# *Olympia's Maid: Reclaiming Black Female Subjectivity* (1992/1994)
# Lorraine O'Grady

*This excerpt is part one, originally published in 1992, of a two-part article, the second part of which was originally published in 1994.*

The female body in the West is not a unitary sign. Rather, like a coin, it has an obverse and a reverse: on the one side, it is white; on the other, non-white or, prototypically, black. The two bodies cannot be separated, nor can one body be understood in isolation from the other in the West's metaphoric construction of "woman." White is what woman is; not-white (and the stereotypes not-white gathers in) is what she had better not be. Even in an allegedly postmodern era, the not-white woman as well as the not-white man are symbolically and even theoretically excluded from sexual difference.[1] Their function continues to be, by their chiaroscuro, to cast the difference of white men and white women into sharper relief.

A kaleidoscope of not-white females, Asian, Native American, Latina, and African, have played distinct parts in the West's theater of sexual hierarchy. But it is the African female who, by virtue of color and feature and the extreme metaphors of enslavement, is at the outermost reaches of "otherness." Thus she subsumes all the roles of the not-white body.

The smiling, bare-breasted African maid, pictured so often in Victorian travel books and *National Geographic* magazine, got something more than a change of climate and scenery when she came here.

Sylvia Arden Boone, in her book *Radiance from the Waters* (1986), on the physical and metaphysical aspects of Mende feminine beauty, says of contemporary Mende: "Mende girls go topless in the village and farmhouse. Even in urban areas, girls are bare-breasted in the house: schoolgirls take off their dresses when they come home, and boarding students are most comfortable around the dormitories wearing only a wrapped skirt."[2]

What happened to the girl who was abducted from her village, then shipped here in chains? What happened to her descendants? Male-fantasy images on rap videos to the contrary, as a swimmer, in communal showers at public pools around the country, I have witnessed black girls and women of all classes showering and shampooing with their bathing suits on, while beside them their white sisters stand unabashedly stripped. Perhaps the progeny of that African maiden feel they must still protect themselves from the centuries-long assault that characterizes them, in the words of the *New York Times* ad placed by a group of African-American women to protest the Clarence Thomas–Anita Hill hearings, as "immoral, insatiable, perverse; the initiators in all sexual contacts—abusive or otherwise."[3]

Perhaps they have internalized and are cooperating with the West's construction of not-white women as not-to-be-seen. How could they/we not be affected by that lingering structure of invisibility, enacted in the myriad codicils of daily life and still enforced by the images of both popular and high culture? How not get the message of what Judith Wilson calls "the legions of black servants who loom in the shadows of European and European-American aristocratic portraiture,"[4] of whom Laura, the professional model that Édouard Manet used for Olympia's maid, is in an odd way only the most famous example? Forget "tonal contrast." We know what she is meant for: she is Jezebel *and* Mammy, prostitute and female eunuch, the two-in-one. When we're through with her inexhaustibly comforting breast, we can use her ceaselessly open cunt. And best of all, she is not a real person, only a robotic servant who is not permitted to make us feel guilty, to accuse us as does the slave in Toni Morrison's *Beloved* (1987). After she escapes from the room where she was imprisoned by a father and son, that outraged woman says: "You couldn't think up what them two done to me."[5] Olympia's maid, like all the other "peripheral Negroes"[6] is a robot conveniently made to disappear into the background drapery.

To repeat: castrata and whore, not madonna and whore. Laura's place is outside what can be conceived of as woman. She is the chaos that must be excised, and it is her excision that stabilizes the West's construct of the female body, for the "femininity" of the white female body is ensured by assigning the not-white to a chaos safely removed from sight. Thus only the white body remains as the object of a voyeuristic, fetishizing male gaze. The not-white body has been made opaque by a blank stare, misperceived in the nether regions of TV.

It comes as no surprise, then, that the imagery of white female artists, including that of the feminist avant-garde, should surround the not-white female body with its own brand of erasure. Much work has been done by black feminist cultural critics (Hazel Carby and bell hooks come immediately to mind) that examines two successive white women's movements, built on the successes of two black revolutions, which clearly shows white women's inability to surrender white skin privilege even to form basic alliances.[7] But more than politics is at stake. A major structure of psychic definition would appear threatened were white women to acknowledge and embrace the sexuality of their not-white "others." How else to explain the treatment by that women's movement icon, Judy Chicago's *Dinner Party* (1973–78) of Sojourner Truth, the lone black guest at the table? When thirty-six of thirty-nine places are set with versions of Chicago's famous "vagina" and recognizable slits have been given to such sex bombs as Queen Elizabeth I, Emily Dickinson, and Susan B. Anthony, what is one to think when Truth, the mother of four, receives the only plate inscribed with a face?[8] Certainly Hortense Spillers is justified in stating that "the excision of the genitalia here is a symbolic castration. By effacing the genitals, Chicago not only abrogates the disturbing sexuality of her subject, but also hopes to suggest that her sexual being did not exist to be denied in the first place."[9]

And yet Michele Wallace is right to say, even as she laments further instances of the disempowerment of not-white women in her essay on *Privilege* (1990), Yvonne Rainer's latest film, that the left-feminist avant-garde, "in foregrounding a political discourse on art and culture," has fostered a climate that makes it "hypothetically possible to publicly review and interrogate that very history of exclusion and racism."[10]

What alternative is there really—in creating a world sensitive to difference, a world where margins can become centers—to a cooperative effort between white women and women and men of color? But cooperation is predicated on sensitivity to differences among ourselves. As Nancy Hartsock has said, "We need to dissolve the false 'we' into its true multiplicity."[11] We must be willing to hear each other and to call each other by our "true-true name."[12]

To name ourselves rather than be named we must first see ourselves. For some of us this will not be easy. So long unmirrored in our true selves, we may have forgotten how we look. Nevertheless, we can't theorize in a void, we must have evidence. And we—I speak only for black women here—have barely begun to articulate our life experience. The heroic recuperative effort by our fiction and nonfiction writers sometimes feel stuck at the moment before the Emancipation Proclamation.[13] It is slow and it is painful. For at the end of every path we take, we find a body that is always already colonized. A body that has been raped, maimed, murdered—that is what we must give a healthy present.

It is no wonder that when Judith Wilson went in search of nineteenth-century nudes by black artists, she found only three statues of non-black children—Edmonia Lewis's *Poor Cupid* (1876); her *Asleep* (1871); and one of the two children in her *Awake* (1872)[14]—though Wilson cautions that, given the limits of current scholarship, more nudes by nineteenth-century blacks may yet surface.[15] Indeed, according to Wilson, the nude, one of high art's favorite categories, has been avoided during most of "the 200-year history of fine art production by North American blacks."[16] Noting exceptions that only prove the rule, that is, individual works by William H. Johnson and Francisco Lord in the thirties and Eldzier Cortor's series of Sea Island nudes in the forties, she calls "the paucity of black nudes in U.S. black artistic production prior to 1960...an unexamined problem in the history of Afro-American art."[17] And why use 1960 as a marker of change? Because, says Wilson, after that date there was a confluence of two different streams: the presence of more, and more aggressive, black fine artists such as Bob Thompson and Romare Bearden, and the political use of the nude as a symbol of "Black Is Beautiful," the sixties slogan of a programmatic effort to establish black ethnicity and achieve psychic transformation.[18]

Neither of these streams, however, begins to deal with what I am concerned with here: the reclamation of the body as a site of black female subjectivity. Wilson hints at part of the problem by subtitling a recent unpublished essay "Bearden's Use of Pornography." An exterior, pornographic view, however loving, will not do any more than will the emblematic "Queen of the Revolution." But though Wilson raises provisional questions about Bearden's montaging of the pornographic image, her concerns are those of the art historian, while mine must be those of the practitioner.[19] When, I ask, do we start to see images of the black female body by black women made as acts of auto-expression, the discrete stage that must immediately precede or occur simultaneously with acts of auto-critique? When, in other words, does the present begin?

Wilson and I agree that, in retrospect, the catalytic moment for the subjective black nude might well be Adrian Piper's *Food for the Spirit* (1971), a private loft performance in which Piper photographed her physical and metaphysical changes during a prolonged period of fasting and reading of Immanuel Kant's *Critique of Pure Reason*.[20] Piper's performance, unpublished and unanalyzed at the time (we did not have the access then that we do now), now seems a paradigm for the willingness to look, to get past embarrassment and retrieve the mutilated body, as Spillers warns we must if we are to gain the clear-sightedness needed to overthrow hierarchical binaries: "Neither the shameface of the embarrassed, nor the not-looking-back of the self-assured is of much interest to us," Spillers writes, "and will not help at all if rigor is our dream."[21]

It is cruelly ironic, of course, that just as the need to establish our subjectivity in preface to theorizing our view of the world becomes most dire, the idea of subjectivity itself has become "problematized." But when we look to see just whose subjectivity has had the ground shifted out from under it in the tremors of postmodernism, we find (who else?) the one to whom Hartsock refers as "the transcendental voice of the Enlightenment" or, better yet, "He Who Theorizes."[22] Well, good riddance to him. We who are inching our way from the margins to the center cannot afford to take his problems or his truths for our own.

Although time may be running out for such seemingly marginal agendas as the establishment of black female subjectivity (the headlines remind us of this every day) and we may feel pressured to move fast, we must not be too conceptually hasty. This is a slow business, as our writers have found out. The work of recuperation continues. In a piece called *Seen* (1990) by the conceptual artist Renee Greene, two of our ancestresses most in need, Saartjie Baartman ("the Hottentot Venus") and Josephine Baker, have been "taken back." Each in her day (early nineteenth and twentieth century, respectively) was the most celebrated European exhibit of exotic flesh. Greene's piece invited the viewer to stand on a stage inscribed with information about the two and, through a "winkie" of eyes in the floor and a shadow screen mounted on the side, to experience how the originals must have felt, pinned and wriggling on the wall. The piece has important attributes: it is above all cool and smart. But from the perspective being discussed here—the establishment of subjectivity—because it is addressed more to the other than to the self and seems to deconstruct the subject just before it expresses it, it may not unearth enough new information.

The question of to whom work is addressed cannot be emphasized too strongly. In the 1970s, African-American women novelists showed how great a leap in artistic maturity could be made simply by turning from their male peers' pattern of "explaining *it* to *them*," as Morrison once put it, to showing how it feels to *us*.[23]

Besides, pleading contains a special trap, as Gayatri Spivak noted in her discussion of the character Christophine in Jean Rhys's *Wide Sargasso Sea*: "No perspective *critical* of imperialism can turn the Other into a self, because the project of imperialism has always already historically refracted what might have been the absolutely Other into a domesticated Other that consolidates the imperialist self."[24] Critiquing *them* does not show who *you* are: it cannot turn you from an object into a subject of history.

The idea bears repeating: self-expression is not a stage that can be bypassed. It is a discrete moment that must precede or occur simultaneously with the deconstructive act. An example may be seen in the work of the painter Sandra Payne. In 1986, at the last show of the now legendary black avant-garde gallery Just Above Midtown in Soho, Payne presented untitled drawings of joyously sexual and sublimely spiritual nudes. The opening reception was one of those where people speak of everything but what is on the walls. We do not yet have the courage to look.

Understandably, Payne went into retreat. Three years later, she produced attenuated mask drawings that, without the hard edge of postmodernism, are a postmodern speech act in the dialogue of mask and masquerade. Without the earlier subjective nudes, she may not have arrived at them.

A year ago, as a performance artist in a crisis of the body (how to keep performing without making aging itself the subject of the work?), I opted for the safety of the wall with a show of photomontages. My choice of the nude was innocent and far from erotic; I wanted to employ a black self stripped of as many layers of acculturation as possible. The one piece in the show with explicitly represented sexuality, *The Clearing* (1991), a diptych in which a black female engaged with a white male, was to me less about sex than it was about culture. It was not possible to remain innocent for long, however. I soon encountered an encyclopedia of problematics concerning the black body: age, weight, condition, not to mention hair texture, features, and skin tone. Especially skin tone. Any male and female side by side on the wall are technically married. How to arrange a quadriptych such as *Gaze* (1991), composed of head-and-shoulder shots of differently hued black men and women? Should I marry the fair woman to the dark man? The dark woman to the fair man? What statements will I be making about difference if I give them mates matching in shade? What will I be saying about the history of class?

There was another problematic, as personal as it was cultural. Which maimed body would be best retrieved as the ground of my biographic experience? Young or middle-aged? Jezebel or Mammy? The woman I was or the woman I am now? And which body hue should I use to generalize my upper-middle-class West Indian-American experience? A black-skinned "ancestress," or the fairer-skinned product of rape? I hedged. In the end, I chose an African-British high-fashion model, London-born but with parents from Sierra Leone. For me, she conveyed important ambiguities: she was black-skinned, but her nude body retained the aura of years of preparation for runway work in Europe. In *The Strange Taxi: From Africa to Jamaica to Boston in 200 Years*, where the subject was hybridism itself, my literal ancestresses, who to some may have looked white, sprouted from a European mansion rolling on wheels down the African woman's back. Although they may have been controversial, I liked the questions those beautifully dressed, proudly erect, ca. World War I women raised, not least of which was how the products of rape could be so self-confident, so poised.

As I wrestled with ever shifting issues regarding which black woman to shoot, I came to understand and sympathize with Lorna Simpson's choice of a unified response in such montages as *Guarded Conditions* (1989), in which a brown-skinned woman in a shapeless white shift is shot from behind—with every aspect of subjectivity both bodily and facial occluded, except the need to cover up itself—and then multiplied. No doubt about it. This multiple woman showers and shampoos in her shift.

But, I tell myself, this cannot be the end. First we must acknowledge the complexity, and then we must surrender to it. Of course, there isn't any final answering of the question, "What happened to that maid when she was brought here?" There is only the process of answering it and the complementary process of allowing each answer to come to the dinner party on its own terms. Each of these processes is just beginning, but perhaps if both continue, the nature of the answers will begin to change and we will all be better off. For if the female body in the West is obverse and reverse, it will not be seen in its integrity—neither side will know itself—until the not-white body has mirrored herself fully.

—

**EXCERPTED FROM LORRAINE O'GRADY, "OLYMPIA'S MAID: RECLAIMING BLACK FEMALE SUBJECTIVITY," 1992/1994, IN AMELIA JONES, ED., *THE FEMINISM AND VISUAL CULTURE READER*, 2ND EDITION (LONDON: ROUTLEDGE, 2010).**

Lorraine O'Grady is an artist and critic whose installations, performances, and texts address issues of diaspora, hybridity, and Black female subjectivity, with special reference to the role these have played in the history of modernism.

1 Hortense J. Spillers, "Interstices: A Small Drama of Words," in *Pleasure and Danger: Exploring Female Sexuality*, ed. Carole S. Vance (Boston: Routledge and Kegan Paul, 1984), 77.

2 Sylvia Arden Boone, *Radiance from the Waters: Ideals of Feminine Beauty in Mende Art* (New Haven, CT: Yale University Press, 1986), 102.

3 "African American Women in Defense of Ourselves," advertisement, *New York Times*, Nov. 17, 1991, 53.

4 Judith Wilson, "Getting Down to Get Over: Romare Bearden's Use of Pornography and the Problem of the Black Female Body in Afro-U.S. Art," in *Black Popular Culture*, ed. Gina Dent (Seattle: Bay Press, 1992), 114.

5 Toni Morrison, *Beloved* (New York: Knopf, 1987), 119.

6 George Nelson Preston, quoted in Wilson, "Getting Down," 114.

7 For an examination of the relationship of black women to the first white feminist movement, see Hazel V. Carby, *Reconstructing Womanhood: The Emergence of the Afro-American Woman Novelist* (New York: Oxford University Press, 1987), chs. 1 and 5, and bell hooks, *Ain't I a Woman: Black Women and Feminism* (Boston: South End Press, 1981). For insights into the problems of black women in the second white feminist movement, see Audre Lorde, "Age, Race, Class, and Sex: Women Redefining Difference," in *Out There: Marginalization and Contemporary Cultures*, ed. Russell Ferguson, Martha Gever, Trinh T. Minh-ha, Cornel West (New York: New Museum of Contemporary Art, 1990), and Bernice Johnson Reagon, "Coalition Politics: Turning the Century," in *Home Girls: A Black Feminist Anthology*, ed. Barbara Smith (New York: Kitchen Table: Women of Color Press, 1983). For problems of women of color in a white women's organization at the start of the third feminist movement, see Lorraine O'Grady on WAC, "Dada Meets Mama," *Artforum* 31, no. 2 (October 1992): 11–12.

8 See Judy Chicago, *The Dinner Party: A Symbol of Our Heritage* (New York: Anchor/Doubleday, 1979).

9 Spillers, "Interstices," 78.

10 Michele Wallace, "Multiculturalism and Oppositionality," in *Afterimage* 19, no. 3 (October 1991):7.

11 Nancy Hartsock, "Rethinking Modernism: Minority vs. Majority Theories," in *Cultural Critique* 7, special issue: "The Nature and Context of Minority Discourse II," ed. Abdul R. JanMohamed and David Lloyd (Fall 1987): 204.

12 See the title story by Merle Hodge in Pamela Mordecai and Betty Wilson, eds., *Her True-True Name* (London: Heinemann Caribbean Writers Series, 1989), 196–202. This anthology is a collection of short stories and novel extracts by women writers from the English-, French-, and Spanish-speaking Caribbean.

**13** The understanding that analysis of the contemporary situation of African-American women is dependent on the imaginative and intellectual retrieval of the black woman's experience under slavery is now so broadly shared that an impressive amount of writings has accumulated. In fiction, a small sampling might include, in addition to Morrison's *Beloved*, Margaret Walker, *Jubilee* (New York: Bantam, 1966); Octavia E. Butler, *Kindred* (1979; reprint, Boston: Beacon Press, 1988); Sherley A. Williams, *Dessa Rose* (New York: William Morrow, 1986); and Gloria Naylor, *Mama Day* (New York: Ticknor and Fields, 1988). For the testimony of slave women themselves, see Harriet A. Jacobs, edited by Jean Fagan Yellin, *Incidents in the Life of a Slave Girl* (Cambridge: Harvard University Press, 1987); *Six Women's Slave Narratives*, the Schomburg Library of Nineteenth-Century Black Women Writers (New York: Oxford University Press, 1988); and Gerda Lerner, ed., *Black Women in White America: A Documentary History* (New York: Vintage Books, 1972). For a historical and sociological overview, see Deborah Gray White, *Ar'n't I a Woman? Female Slaves in the Plantation South* (New York: W.W. Norton, 1985).

**14** Wilson, "Getting Down," 121, note 13.

**15** Ibid., 114

**16** Ibid.

**17** Ibid.

**18** Judith Wilson, telephone conversation with the author, January 21, 1992.

**19** Wilson, "Getting Down," 116–18.

**20** Adrian Piper, "Food for the Spirit, July 1971," in *High Performance 13* (spring 1981). This was the first chronicling of *Food* with accompanying images. The nude image from this performance first appeared in Piper's retrospective catalogue; Jane Farver, *Adrian Piper: Reflections 1967–87* (New York: Alternative Museum, April 18–May 30, 1987).

**21** Hortense J. Spillers, "Mama's Baby, Papa's Maybe: An American Grammar Book," in *Diacritics* 17, no. 2 (summer 1987): 68.

**22** Hartsock, "Rethinking Modernism," 196, 194.

**23** Toni Morrison, in Charles Ruas, "Toni Morrison's Triumph," an interview in *Soho News*, 11–17 March 1981, 12.

**24** Gayatri Chakravorty Spivak, "Three Women's Texts and a Critique of Imperialism," in *"Race," Writing, and Difference*, ed. Henry Louis Gates Jr. (Chicago: University of Chicago Press, 1986), 272.

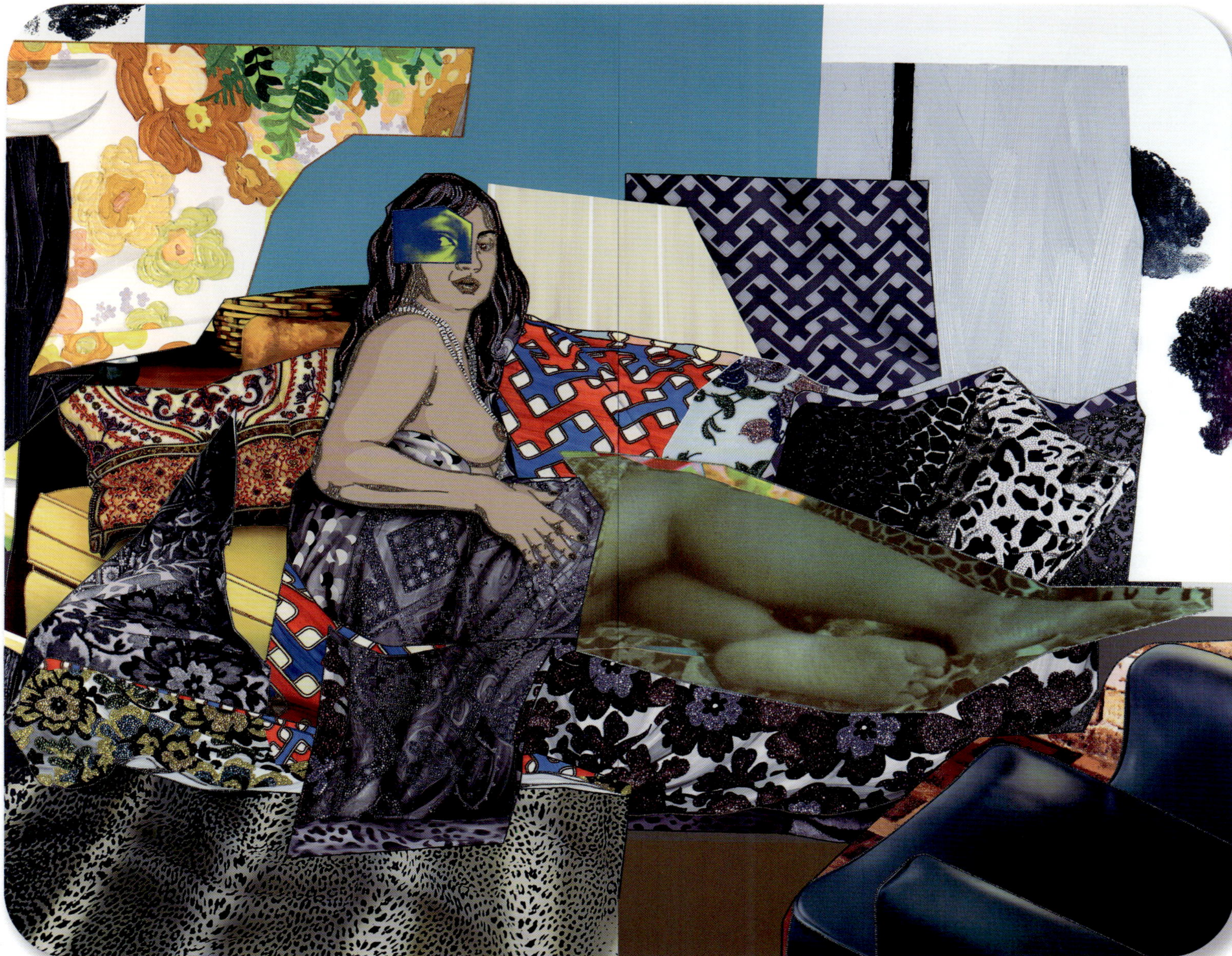

SHINIQUE: NOW I KNOW, 2015

# *The Color Purple* (1982)
# Alice Walker

DEAR GOD,

Mr. _____ finally come right out an ast for Nettie hand in marriage. But He won't let her go. He say she too young, no experience. Say Mr. _____ got too many children already. Plus What about the scandal his wife cause when somebody kill her? And what about all this stuff he hear bout Shug Avery? What bout that?

I ast our new mammy bout Shug Avery. What it is? I ast. She don't know but she say she gon fine out.

She do more then that. She git a picture. The first one of a real person I ever seen. She say Mr. _____ was taking somethin out his billfold to show Pa an it fell out an slid under the table. Shug Avery was a woman. The most beautiful woman I ever saw. She more pretty then my mama. She bout ten thousand times more prettier then me. I see her there in furs. Her face rouge. Her hair like somethin tail. She grinning with her foot up on somebody motocar. Her eyes serious tho. Sad some.

I ast her to give me the picture. An all night long I stare at it. An now when I dream, I dream of Shug Avery. She be dress to kill, whirling and laughing.

—



Alice Walker is an internationally celebrated writer, poet, and activist whose books include seven novels, four collections of short stories, four children's books, and volumes of essays and poetry. She won the Pulitzer Prize in Fiction and the National Book Award in 1983 for *The Color Purple*.

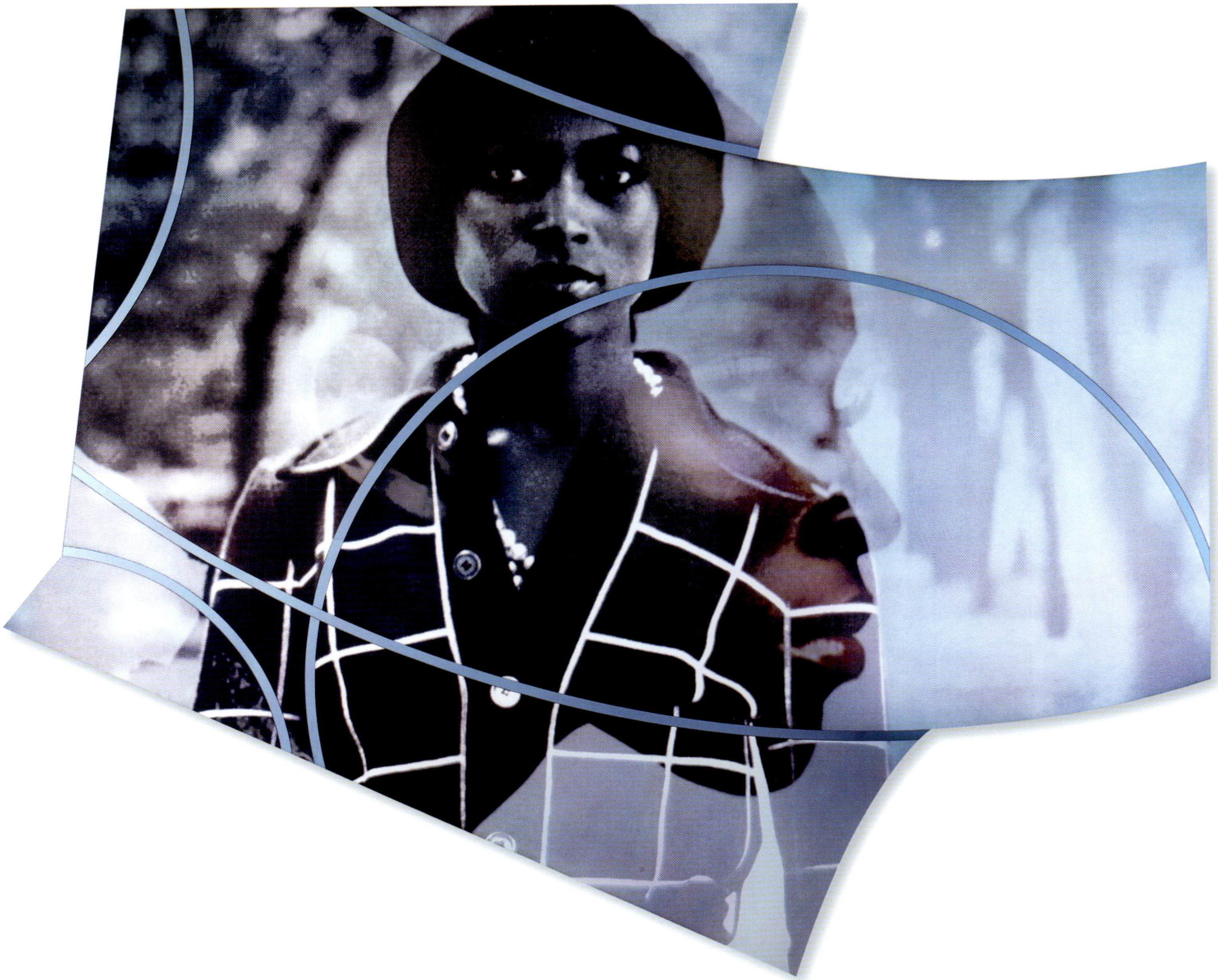



**NAOMI SIMS #2, 2016**

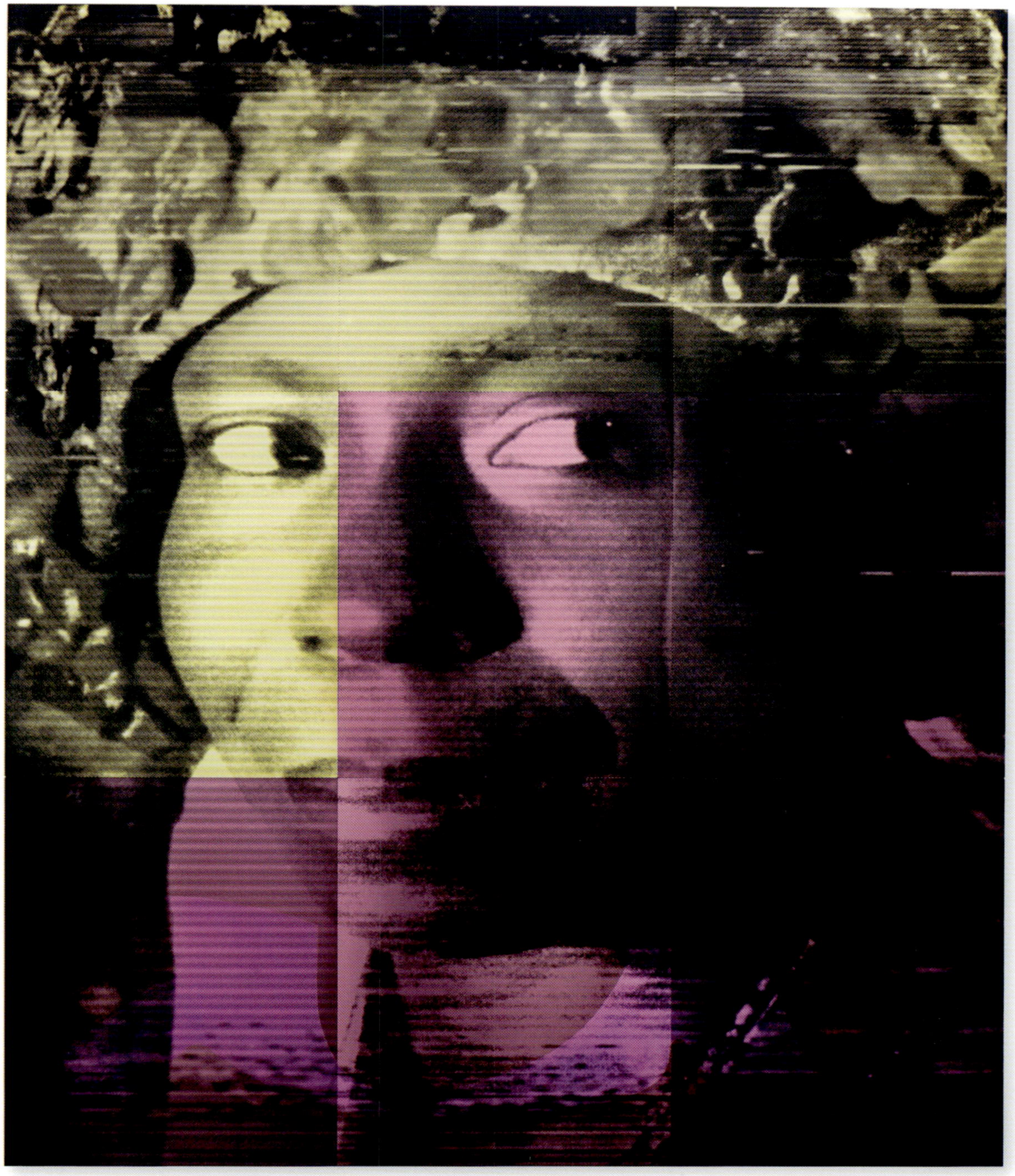

**BLUES, 2016**

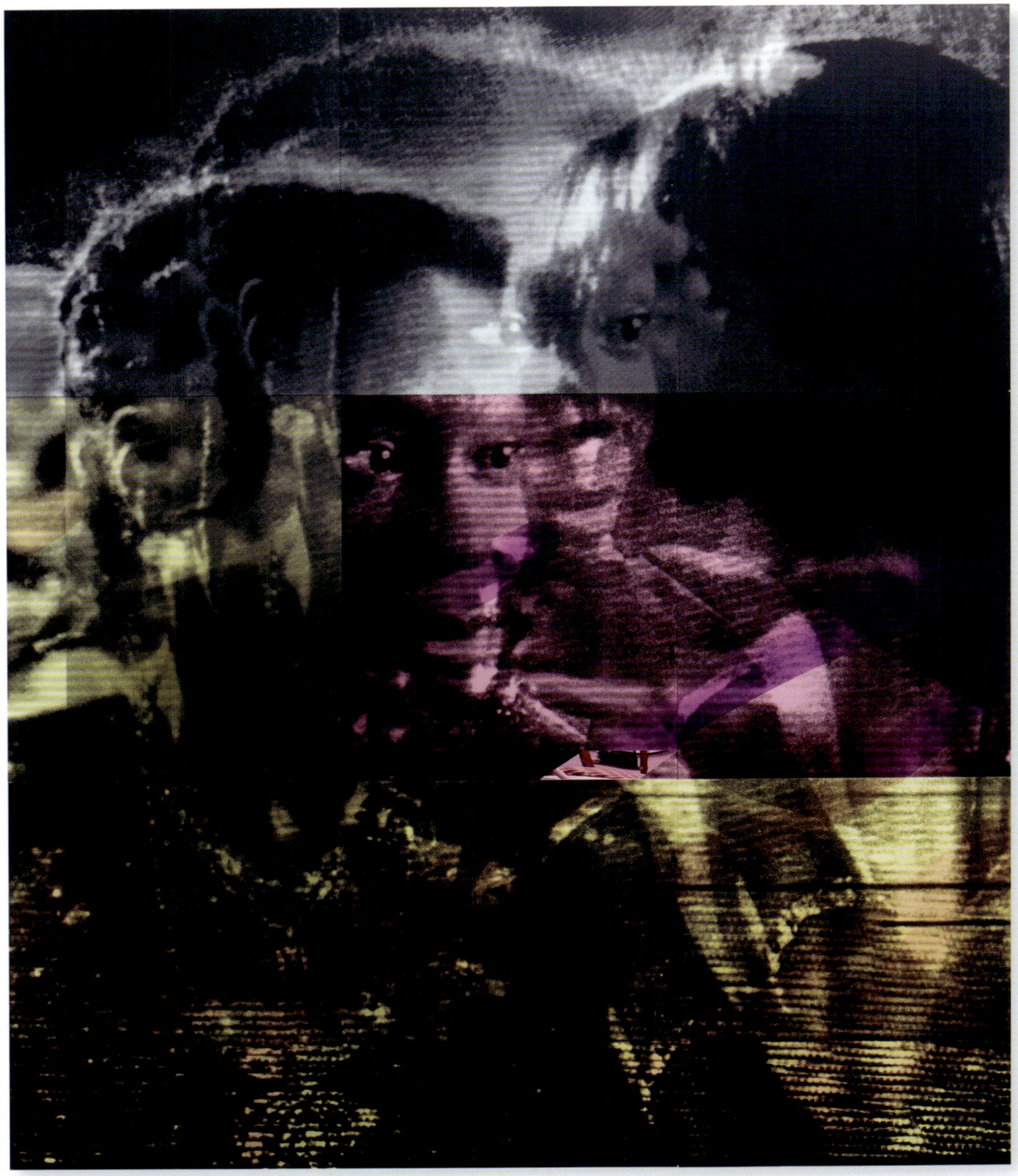



**SHUG KISSES CELIE, 2016**

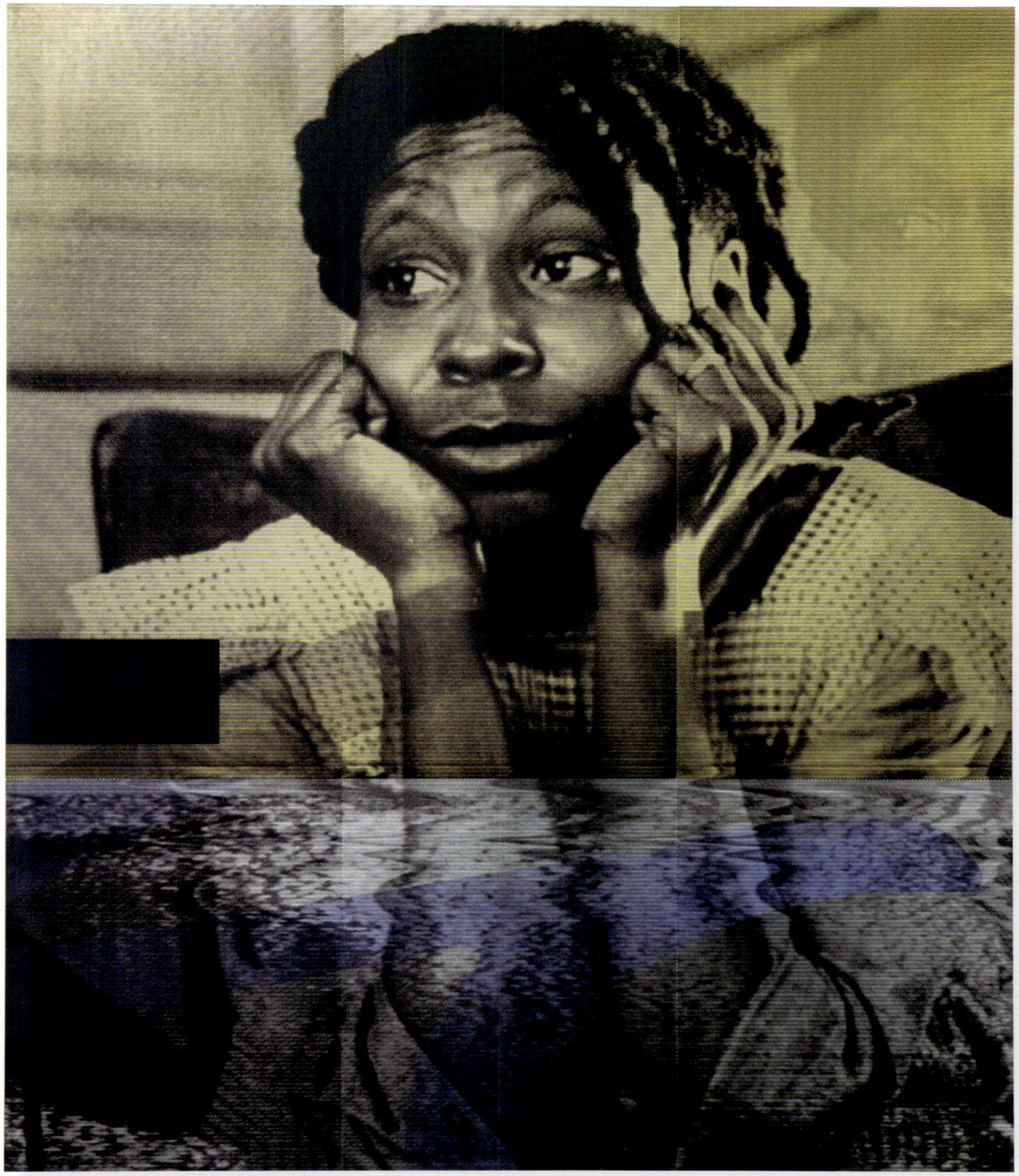

SISTER: SHUG AVERY BREAKFAST, 2016

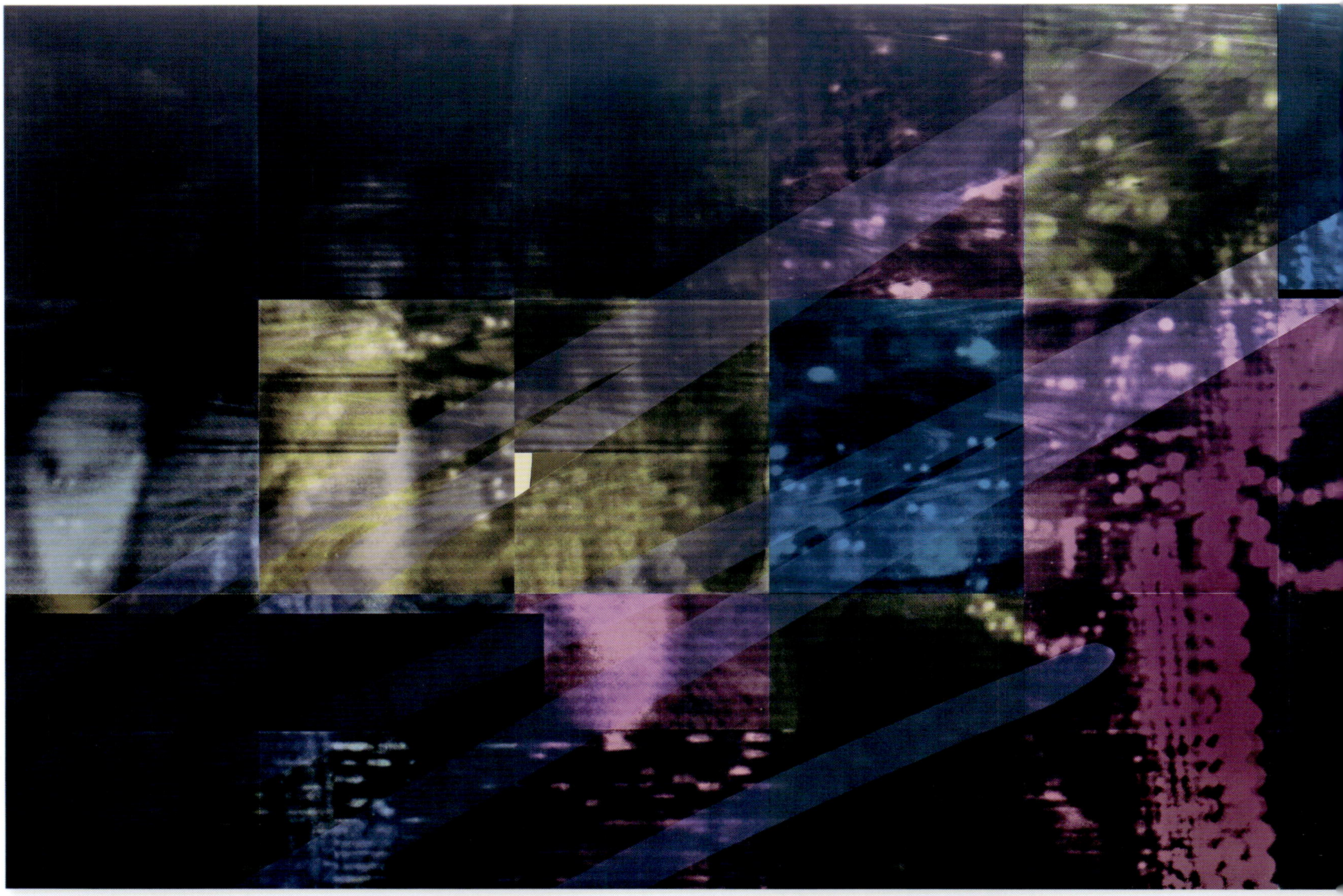



MS. CELIE'S BLUES, 2016

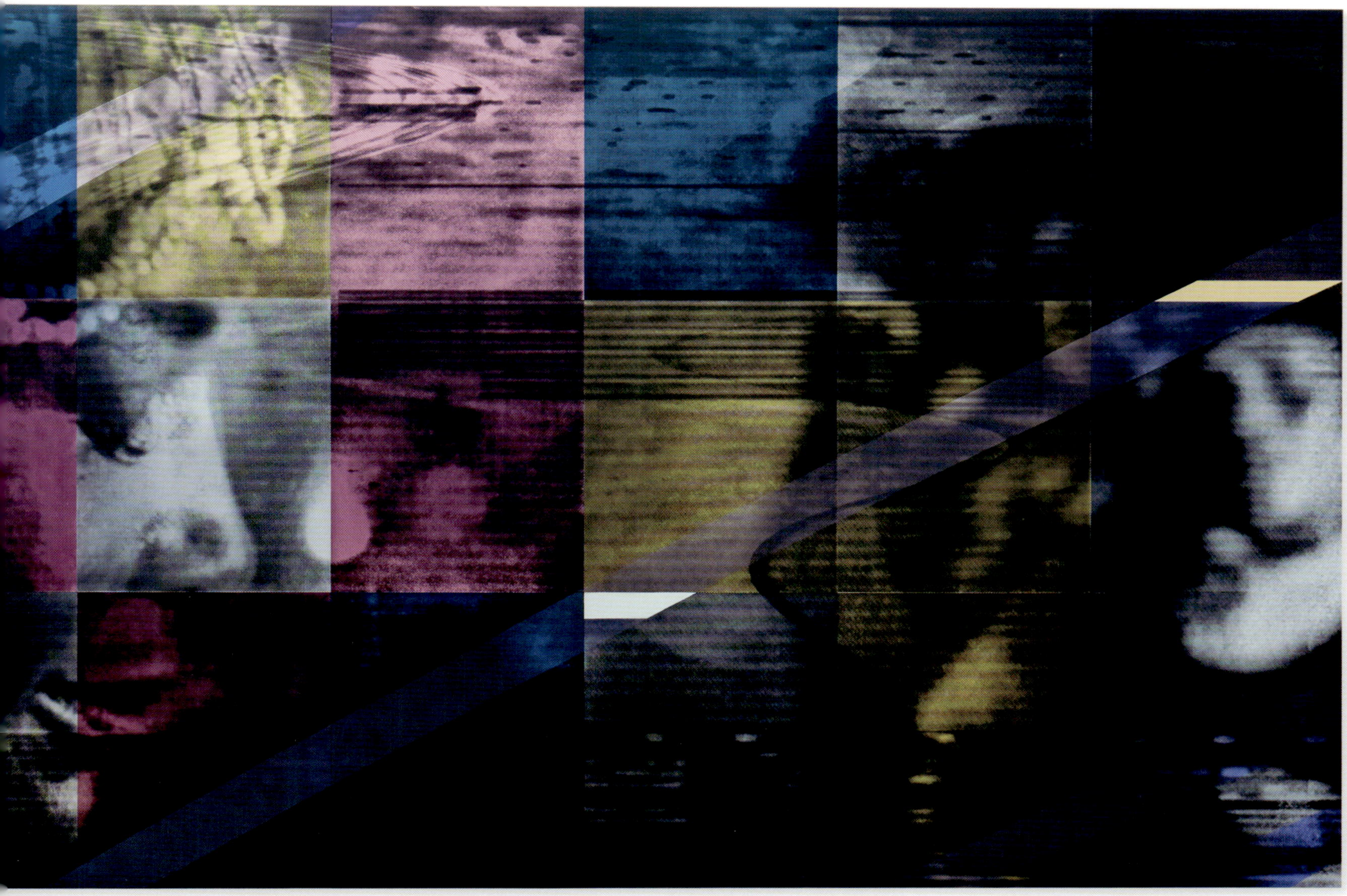

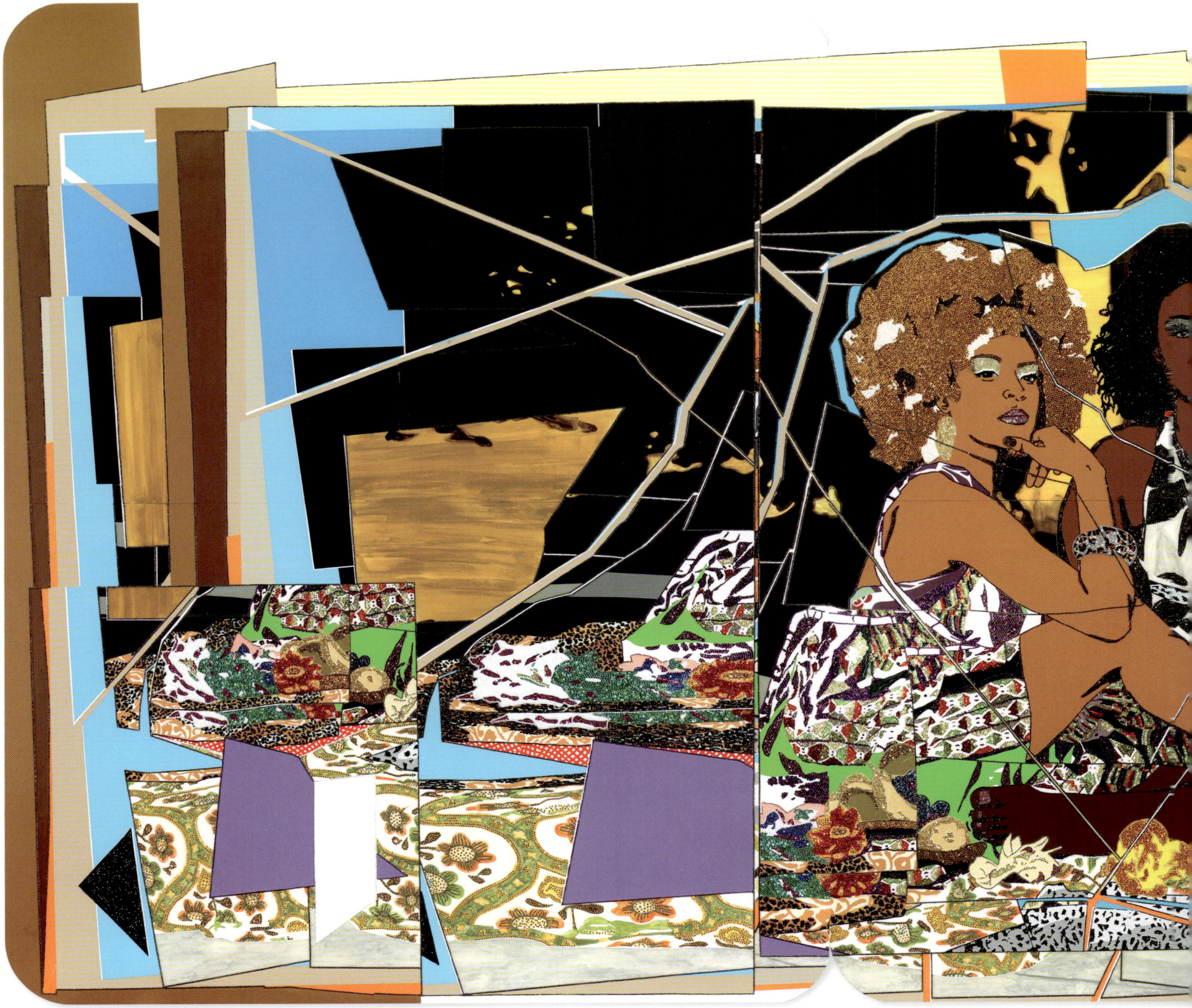



LE DÉJEUNER SUR L'HERBE: LES TROIS FEMMES NOIRES, 2010

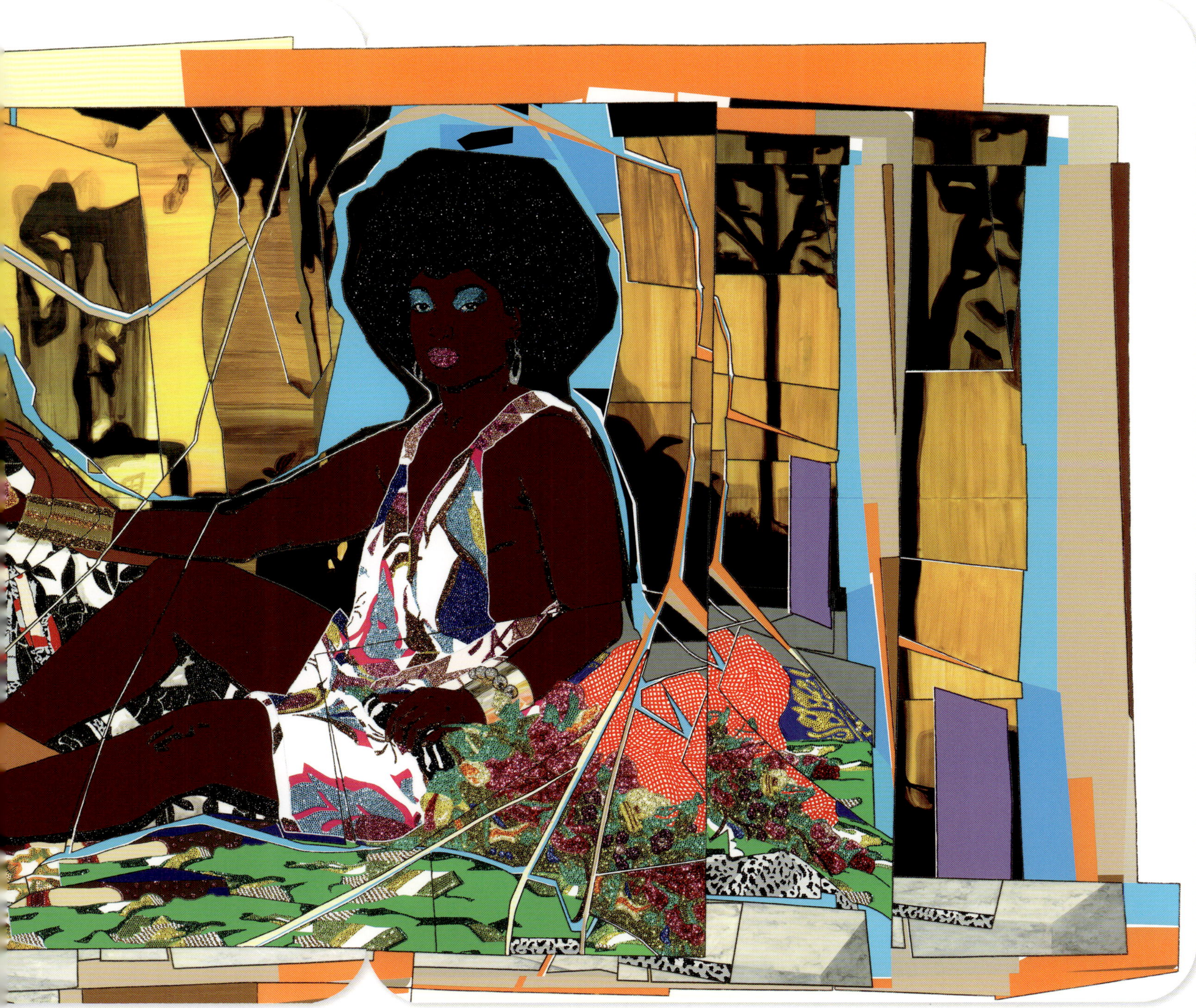

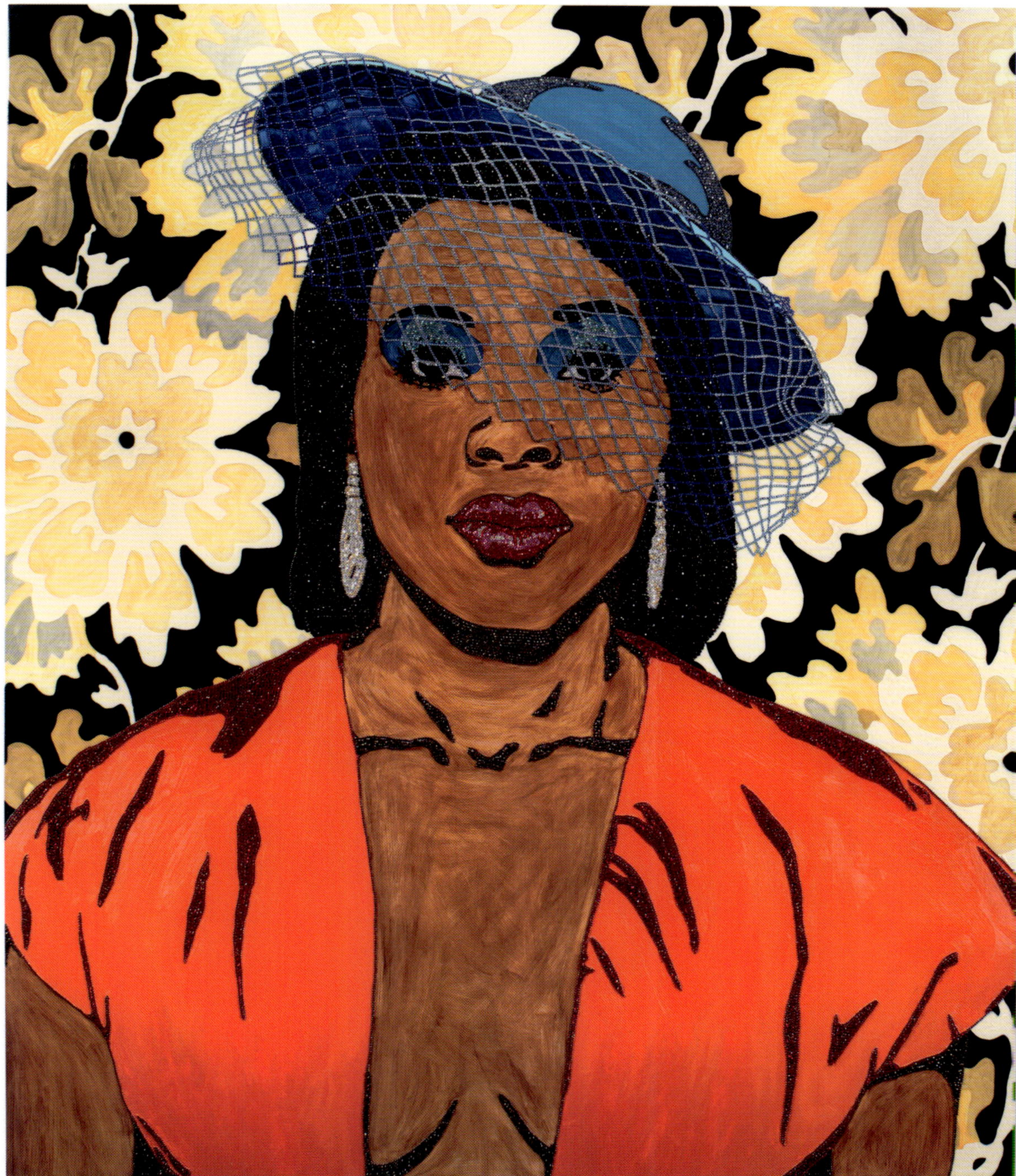

**QUSUQUZAH, UNE TRÈS BELLE NÉGRESSE #3, 2012**

# *Americanah* (2013)
# Chimamanda Ngozi Adichie

Finally, Aisha finished with her customer and asked what colour Ifemelu wanted for her hair attachments.

"Colour four."

"Not good colour," Aisha said promptly.

"That's what I use."

"It look dirty. You don't want colour one?"

"Colour one is too black, it looks fake," Ifemelu said, loosening her headwrap. "Sometimes I use colour two, but colour four is closest to my natural colour."

Aisha shrugged, a haughty shrug, as though it was not her problem if her customer did not have good taste. She reached into a cupboard, brought out two packets of attachments, checked to make sure they were both the same colour.

She touched Ifemelu's hair. "Why you don't have relaxer?"

"I like my hair the way God made it."

"But how you comb it? Hard to comb," Aisha said.

Ifemelu had brought her own comb. She gently combed her hair, dense, soft and tightly coiled, until it framed her head like a halo. "It's not hard to comb if you moisturize it properly," she said, slipping into the coaxing tone of the proselytizer that she used whenever she was trying to convince other black women about the merits of wearing their hair natural. Aisha snorted; she clearly could not understand why anybody would choose to suffer through combing natural hair, instead of simply relaxing it. She sectioned out Ifemelu's hair, plucked a little attachment from the pile on the table and began deftly to twist.

"It's too tight," Ifemelu said. "Don't make it tight." Because Aisha kept twisting to the end, Ifemelu thought that perhaps she had not understood, and so Ifemelu touched the offending braid and said,"Tight, tight."

Aisha pushed her hand away. "No. No. Leave it. It good."

"It's tight!" Ifemelu said. "Please loosen it."

Mariama was watching them. A flow of French came from her. Aisha loosened the braid.

"Sorry," Mariama said. "She doesn't understand very well."

But Ifemelu could see, from Aisha's face, that she understood very well. Aisha was simply a true market woman, immune to the cosmetic niceties of American customer service. Ifemelu imagined her working in a market in Dakar, like the braiders in Lagos who would blow their noses and wipe their hands on their wrappers, roughly jerk their customers' heads to position them better, complain about how full or how hard or how short the hair was, shout out to passing women, while all the time conversing too loudly and braiding too tightly.

—



Chimamanda Ngozi Adichie is the author of *Americanah*, which won the National Book Critics Circle Award and was named one of the *New York Times* Top Ten Best Books of 2013, as well as the novels *Purple Hibiscus* and *Half of a Yellow Sun*, the short-story collection *The Thing Around Your Neck*, the book-length essay *We Should All Be Feminists*, and the treatise *Dear Ijeawele, or A Feminist Manifesto in Fifteen Suggestions*. She was the recipient of the PEN Pinter Prize in 2018.

# *We Are Ugly, But We Are Here* (2005)
## Edwidge Danticat

One of the first people murdered on our land was a queen. Her name was Anacaona and she was an Arawak Indian. She was a poet, dancer, and even a painter. She ruled over the western part of an island so lush and green that the Arawaks called it Ayiti, land of high. When the Spaniards came from across the sea to look for gold, Anacaona was one of their first victims. She was raped and killed and her village pillaged. Anacaona's land is now often called the poorest country in the Western hemisphere, a place of continuous political unrest. Thus, for some, it is easy to forget that this land was the first Black republic, home to the first people of African descent to uproot slavery and create an independent nation in 1804.

I was born under Haiti's dictatorial Duvalier regime. When I was four, my parents left Haiti to seek a better life in the United States. I must admit that their motives were more economic than political, but as anyone who knows Haiti will tell you, economics and politics are intrinsically related; who is in power determines to a great extent whether or not people will eat.

I am thirty-four years old now and have spent more than two-thirds of my life in the United States. My most vivid childhood memories of Haiti involve sudden power failures, "blakawouts," we called them. During blackouts, I couldn't read, study, or watch television, so I'd sit around a candle or a kerosene lamp and listen to stories from the elders in the house.

My grandmother was an old country woman who always felt displaced in the capital where we lived. She had nothing but her patched-up quilts and her stories to console her. She was the one who told me about Anacaona. I used to share a room with her, and I was in the room with her when she died. She was over a hundred years old. She died with her eyes wide open; I was the one who closed them. I still miss the countless stories she told us. However, I accepted her death very easily because death was always around.

As a little girl, I attended more than my share of funerals. My uncle and legal guardian was a Baptist minister and his family was expected to attend every funeral he presided over. I went to all the funerals in the same white lace dress. Perhaps it was because I attended so many funerals that I have such a strong feeling that death is not the end, that the people we put in the ground are going off to live somewhere else. But at the same time, I believe they will always hover around to watch over us and guide us through our journeys.

When I was eight, my uncle's brother-in-law went on a long journey to cut cane in the Dominican Republic. He came back deathly ill. I remember his wife twirling feathers inside his nostrils and rubbing black pepper on his upper lip to make him sneeze. She strongly believed that if he sneezed, he would live. At night, it was my job to watch the sky above the house for signs of falling stars. In rural Haitian lore, when a star falls out of the sky, it means someone will die. A star did fall out of the sky and he did die.

I have childhood memories of Jean-Claude "Baby Doc" Duvalier and his wife, Michèle, racing by in their Mercedes-Benz and throwing money out of the window to the very poor children in our neighborhood. The children would nearly kill each other trying to catch a coin or a glimpse of Baby Doc and Michèle. One Christmas, it was announced on the radio that the First Lady would be giving away free toys at the palace. My cousins and I went and were nearly crushed in the mob of children who flooded the palace lawns.

These stories and memories bring the questions always buzzing to my head. What is my place now in all of this? What was my grandmother's place? What is the legacy of the daughters of Anacaona, the daughters of Haiti?

Watching the news reports, it is often hard to tell whether there are real living and breathing women in conflict-stricken places like Haiti. The evening news broadcasts only allow us brief glimpses of presidential coups, rejected boat people, and sabotaged elections. The women's stories never manage to make the front page. But they do exist.

Over the years, I have known women who, when the soldiers came to their homes in Haiti, would tell their daughters to lie still and play dead. I once met a woman whose sister was shot in her pregnant stomach because she was wearing a t-shirt with an "anti-military image." I know a mother who was arrested and beaten for working with a pro-democracy group. Her body remains laced with scars where the soldiers put out their cigarettes on her flesh. At night, this woman still smells the ashes of the cigarette butts that were stuffed, lit, inside her nostrils. In the same jail cell, she watched as paramilitary "attachés" raped her fourteen-year-old daughter at gunpoint. When mother and daughter took a tiny boat to the United States, the mother had no idea that her daughter was pregnant. Nor did she know that her child had gotten the HIV virus from one of the paramilitary men who had raped her. The offspring of the rape, her grandchild, was named Anacaona after the Arawak queen, because that family of women is from Léogane, the same region where Anacaona was murdered, the same region where my grandmother was born.

The infant Anacaona has a face which no longer shows any trace of Indigenous blood, but her story echoes some of the first incidents of bloodshed in a land that has seen much more than its share.

There is a Haitian saying that might upset the aesthetic sensibilities of some women. *"Nou léd, Nou la,"* it says. "We are ugly, but we are here." Like the modesty that is common in rural Haitian culture, this saying makes a deeper claim for poor Haitian women than maintaining beauty, be it skin-deep or otherwise. For women like my grandmother, what is worth celebrating is the fact that we are here, that against all the odds, we exist. To women like my grandmother, who greeted each other with this saying when they met along a trail in the countryside, the very essence of life lies in survival. It is always worth reminding our sisters that we have lived yet another day to answer the roll call of an often painful and very difficult life. It is in this spirit that to this day a woman remembers to name her child Anacaona, a name which resonates both the splendor and agony of a past that haunts so many women, and men, today.

When they were enslaved, our foremothers believed that when they died their spirits would return to Africa, most specifically to a peaceful land we call Ginen, where gods and goddesses live. The women who came before me were women who spoke half of one language and half another. They spoke the French and Spanish of their colonizers mixed in with their own African language. These women seemed to be speaking in tongue when they prayed to their old gods, the ancient African spirits. Even though they were afraid that their old deities would no longer understand them, they invented a new language with which to describe their new surroundings, a language from which colorful phrases blossomed to fit the desperate circumstances. When these women greeted each other, they found themselves speaking in codes.

—How are we today, sister?
—I am ugly, but I am here.

These days, many of my sisters are greeting each other far away from the lands where they first learned to speak in tongues. Many have made it to other shores, after traveling endless miles on the high seas, on rickety boats that almost took their lives. On October 29, 2002, a woman, weakened by a long ocean journey, spotted land and leapt into the shallow tide. Others followed, including little girls and boys who risked breaking an arm rather than separate from their parents. These are only some of the thousands who reach American shores each year, only to be rounded up, shackled, and taken away, often sent back where they came from.

Eleven years ago, a mother jumped into the sea when she discovered that her baby daughter had died in her arms on a journey that she had hoped would take them to a brighter future. Mother and child, they sank to the bottom of an ocean which already holds millions of souls from the middle passage, the holocaust of the slave trade. That woman's sacrifice moved many of us to tears, even while it reminded us of a slew of past sacrifices made previously for all of us, so that we could be here.

The past is full of examples of our foremothers showing such deep trust in the sea that they would jump off slave ships and let the waves embrace them. They believed that the sea was the beginning and the end of all things, the road to freedom and their entrance to Ginen. These women, women like my grandmother who taught me the story of Anacaona, the queen, have been part of the very construction of my being ever since I was a little girl.

My grandmother believed that if a life is lost, then another one springs up replanted somewhere else, the next life even stronger than the last. She believed that no one really dies as long as someone remembers, someone who will acknowledge that this person had, in spite of everything, been here. We are part of an endless circle, the daughters of Anacaona. We have stumbled, but have not fallen. We are ill-favored, but still we endure. Every once in a while, we must scream this as far as the wind can carry our voices: "*Nou led, nou la!*" We are ugly, but we are here!

And here to stay.

—

**REPRINTED FROM *WOMEN WRITING RESISTANCE: ESSAYS ON LATIN AMERICA AND THE CARIBBEAN*, ED. JENNIFER BROWDY DE HERNANDEZ (CAMBRIDGE: SOUTH END PRESS, 2005), 23–27.**

Edwidge Danticat is a Haitian-American novelist and short-story writer. Her books include *Breath, Eyes, Memory* (an Oprah Book Club selection), *Krik? Krak!* (a National Book Award finalist), *The Farming of Bones*, *The Dew Breaker*, *Create Dangerously*, and *Claire of the Sea Light*.

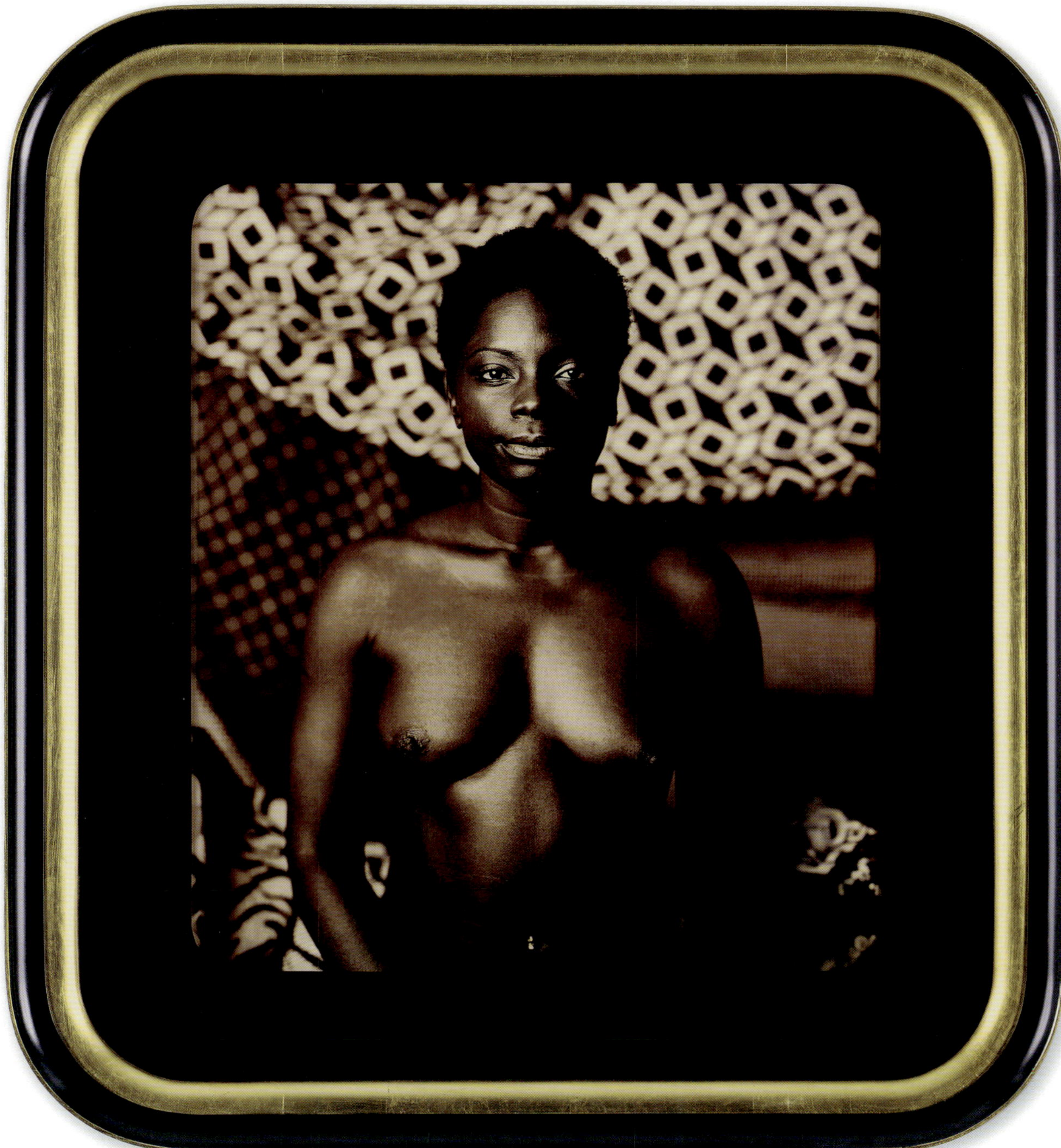

COURBET #4 (MARIE: CENTERED), 2011

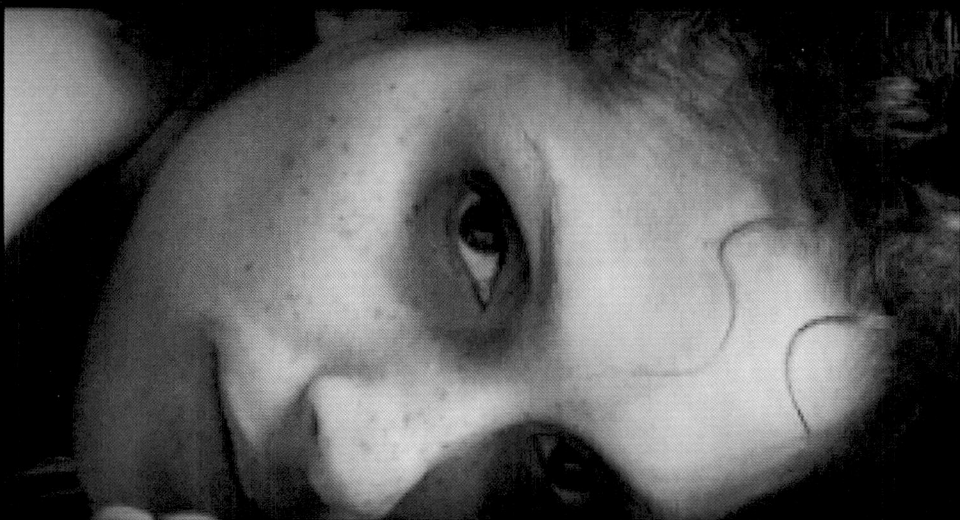

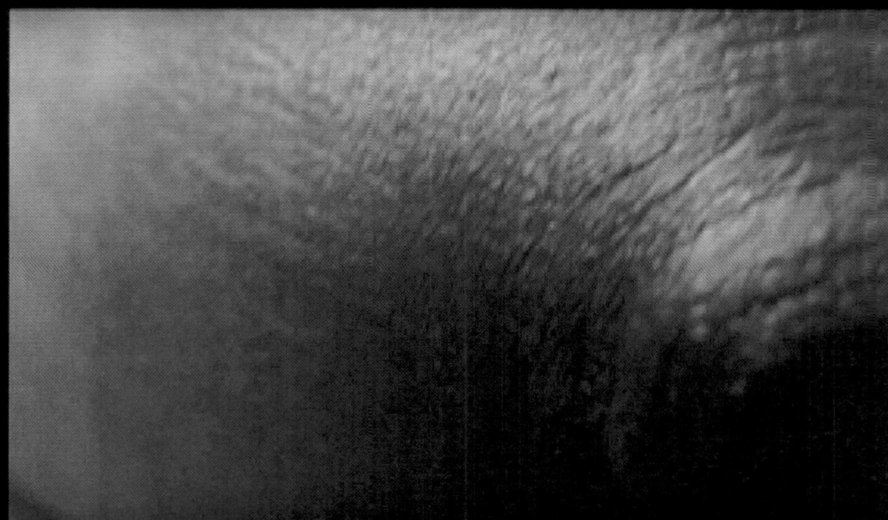



JE T'AIME DEUX, 2014

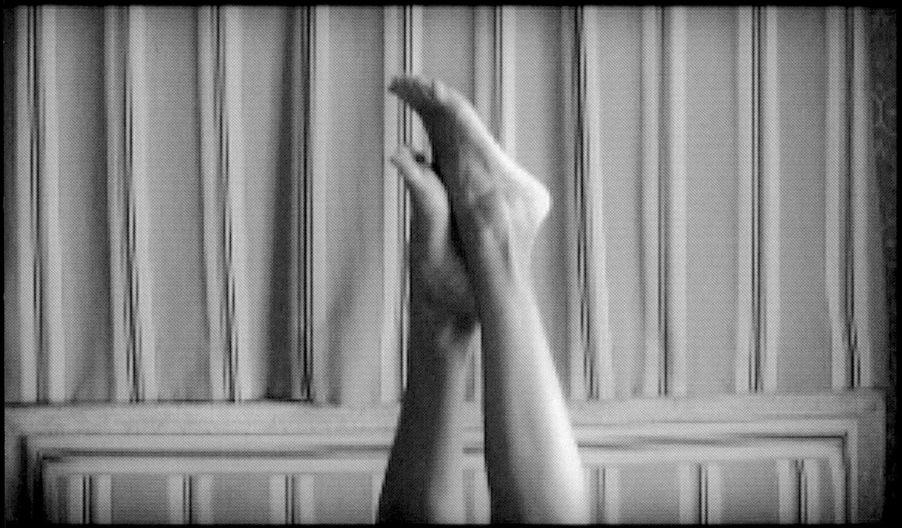

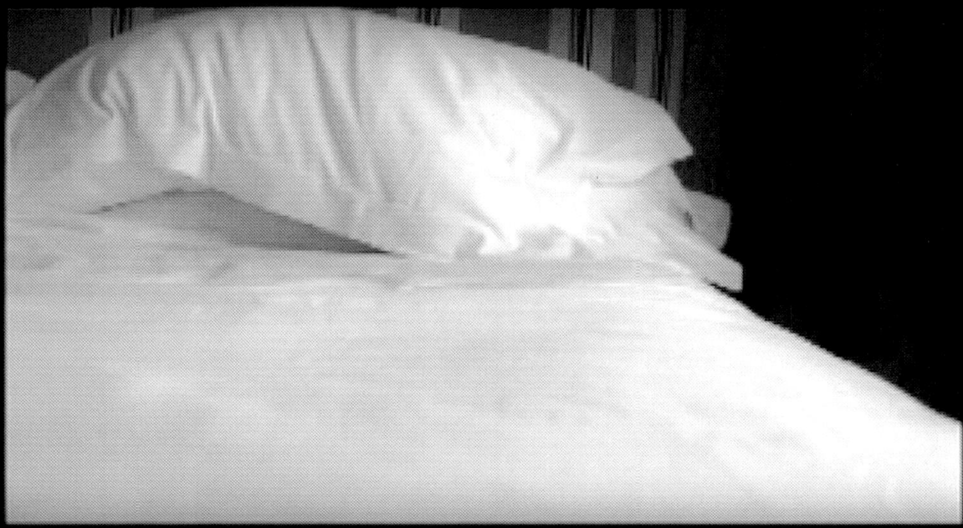

## *Sisterhood Is a Behaviour: Mickalene Thomas's Restaging of Womanhood*

Antwaun Sargent

John Coltrane's famous Cousin Mary once said Trane played the way he did because he wanted to sing like the sisters in the church but couldn't.
—Greg Tate[1]

I wish my pussy could live
in a different shape and get
some goddamn respect.
—Morgan Parker[2]

Mickalene Thomas's intimate Black Is Beautiful scene, the painting *Le déjeuner sur l'herbe: Les trois femmes noires* (2010) (pages 50–51), evokes and disrupts Édouard Manet's notorious 1863 oil painting, *Le déjeuner sur l'herbe* (page 19), to present a profound and aspirational image of Black women's connections to history, art, and each other. Thomas's work has always been a bright alarm sounding in the midst of representational darkness; since 2000, it has provided alternatives to a historical and present-day nightmare for women in general and Black women in particular.

Like many of Thomas's photographs, canvases, and videos, this painting features three Black women—Moniladae, Din, and Qusuquzah—as iconic signifiers. The three women, dressed in glittering, rhinestone-encrusted sundresses that complement their equally radiant eyeshadow and perfectly coiffed hair, make their own statements about Black Power. These three, unlike other women in the history of art, are given pride of place and real respect. They sit like monuments in the middle of the panel, and this centrality, combined with their direct gazes, emphasizes their importance and power. Moniladae holds her hand to her chin, Din reclines, and Qusuquzah, evoking biblical imagery and thus acknowledging she is aware of her historic nakedness, holds what appears to be forbidden fruit. Despite the distorting forces of art and history, these women are shown as desirable; beings who know what they want, introducing a new negotiable tension between how art and history have represented them and how they might present themselves. This tension is heightened by the care taken in the construction of the image's surface, embellished with rhinestone and glitter—Thomas's signature materials, long considered to be feminine, which deftly call to mind craft, pointillism, dot painting, and the glam of disco.

Thomas's bold and empowered envisioning of Black women is rooted in sisterhood, a refusal to believe in the invisibility of Black women—which is to say, in the invisibility of herself. This seeing and self-validation dates back to her childhood. "I grew up with a lot of brothers and I don't have any sisters," she says, "so for me it's really important to develop my sisterhood."[3] The images of women in Thomas's art embody a sense of sisterhood in all its diversity and defiance, and this sense is palpable and sexy in *Le déjeuner sur l'herbe: Les trois femmes noires*—you want to sit with them, look like them.

The display of sisterhood grows more profound as a reappropriation of and salvo against Manet's *Le déjeuner sur l'herbe*. Manet's painting is of two fully dressed white men sitting in a park with a naked white woman in the foreground. In the background a scantily dressed white woman looks at the ground in a state of bewilderment, as if she has lost something—perhaps a sense of self and sisterhood! Manet's picture affirms a different truth: Women, when without power or when presumed to be without desire, are seen as servile objects to be protected, to be fucked, to be silenced.

In contrast to the women in the Manet painting, the Black women in Thomas's painting are notably chic, commanding, and clothed. We see a rejection of the male gaze, as the painting borrows from Manet to weaken his position of power as painter of women. The Thomas portrait conveys a complex and empowered notion of race, gender, sexuality, and beauty, deliberately envisioning the power of womanhood as sisterhood.

Thomas also restages her women, moving the scene from the grass of Manet's luncheon to a safe space: a Black family's 1970s-era living room. The most public of private spaces and one often styled by Black women, the living room operates within Thomas's work as a metaphor for freedom, subjectivity, and the expression (silenced elsewhere) of Black sisterhood. It is an elaborate and fashionable space, a site where sisterhood happens, and is shaped by a heartfelt fusing of facts and fictions. In this work and others, Thomas's use of collage suggests her subjects are presented in makeshift spaces, a collection of histories informed by women. Yet these are not just spaces for ordinary tableaux. Clashes of patterns and fabrics and painted blocks of colour have a transcendent effect, moving the subjects into position in "retablo, with its connotations of the sacred," as the poet and essayist Elizabeth Alexander argues in *The Black Interior*.[4] Alexander elaborates:

> The living room is where we see black imagination made visual, a private space that inevitably reverberates against the garish public images usually out of our control. What does how we arrange interior space say about how we live? And what does that say about who we are?...The will to beauty, the will to fantasy, the will to wish, the power to wish, wish translated to action, all are identified and enacted through the power of the visual. The living room is the space where this "takes place."[5]

According to art historian Denise Murrell, Thomas's reformulation of the Black female figure in elaborate living rooms "links her with contemporary artists"—Lorraine O' Grady, Carrie Mae Weems, Lorna Simpson, and Deana Lawson, among others—"who address a need, expressed by Lorraine O'Grady, for 'images of the black female body by black women made as acts of auto-expression, the discrete stage that must immediately precede or occur simultaneously with acts of auto-critique."[6] The need for images of Black women by Black women takes on considerably more urgency considering the ways their image has been abused throughout history.

The poet Robin Coste Lewis lays bare the unique status of the Black female body in *Voyage of the Sable Venus*. In her eighty-page narrative poem, culled from descriptions of the Black femme figure found in images on the walls and in the wall labels and catalogues of museums dating back to 36,000 BCE, she writes:

> *Gone!*
> *An Historical Romance of Civil War as It Occurred*
> *Between the Dusky Thighs of a Young Negress and Her Heart Detail*
>
> *(From a Series of the Four Continents Allegory of America, or Paraí en Brasil—*
>
> *Mil Años de Creatividad:*
>
> Alabama Sketchbook:
> Seated Negro Woman Looking
> To the left, drawing
>
> half-length image of a Young Negro Woman
> Wearing a Dress with an Empire.

Waistline and pearl,
Earrings and necklace, and holding
a basket of flowers over her left arm, painting

The Slaves escaping through
the swamp, The Slave watching
her pursuers in for e—

Ground Black Woman walking in front
of a Board Fence Background Plantation House
and Outbuilding (or Slave Quarters).

In a Grove of Trees Slave Woman wearing a Runaway.
Collar with Two Children, emaciated.
Negro Man eating Dead.[7]

The most important relationships reveal themselves clearly in Thomas's work: that is, the women's relationships to each other, sisterhood. In the Manet work the women share race and gender but not much else; Thomas's women's bodies are turned toward each other, their faces toward the viewer, sitting in a scene pulled from fragments of pensées, living rooms, and nature, fragments that suggest the chaos of both personal and collective history. Within that chaos, the tableau of Moniladae, Din, and Qusuquzah serenely sitting in sisterhood becomes a masterful image of power rooted in togetherness and rebellion, one that rewrites histories of absence. The women's unbreakable gazes seem collective in nature, as if they are staring at you from the shared well of experience, of blood or of struggle. The gazes are a reminder of the way aunties have stared for centuries, unafraid but with a deep vulnerability: They want you to see them and to see more.

To get the expressiveness of Moniladae, Din, and Qusuquzah's eyes just right for the painting, Thomas recontextualized an earlier photograph. She says, "The photograph defines my practice,"[8] because the photograph captures a truth concerning the gazes of Black women that contributes to making her paintings more accurate. "There's something about a photograph that I can never get in a painting," she admits. "I think there's something about the gaze in a photograph that is completely shifted in a painting because the artist can change the gaze a little."[9]

The gaze of sisterhood that appears throughout Thomas's art recurs even in her works of individual Black women, on the canvas or in photographs and video. *Portrait of Marie* (2015) (page 29) is a collage combining a black and white photo of the sitter with sections painted in shades of brown and blue, casting her face against a boldly patterned backdrop. It suggests not a deconstruction of Black femme identity, but rather a composite of every Black woman, past and present. It suggests that a portrait can reveal or present many selves at once; and that beauty is common and must constantly be reimagined. In queering our notion of beauty, Thomas suggests it is an accessible site, a challenge to be overcome, for varied Black female expression.

The positioning of Marie's eyes, in a way that suggests she simultaneously gazes at and past you, seems to play with power, claiming what has not been hers historically. The gaze rejects traditional heterosexist associations that exclude the sisters that come to you informally, outside of blood and because of it. It's a sisterhood that is captured in the way some women tell their daughters "Think of me as a sister"—which is to say, "*Trust me* beyond tradition." Sisterhood, as Thomas has captured it, is a forged and abiding solidarity, a commitment to survival. It is closely aligned with the suggestion, from Black feminist scholar bell hooks, that if we are interested in a freedom beyond what we have come to know under patriarchy and white supremacy, then "we must learn the true meaning and value of Sisterhood." This sisterhood, according to hooks, is not primarily about a "common oppression" that has produced occasional support. It is a reflection of the dignity of "sustained on-going commitment"[10] to each other, in what Thomas has called "mirror images."[11]

hooks has rightly written, "The black body has always received attention within the framework of white supremacy, as racist/sexist iconography has been deployed to perpetuate notions of innate biological inferiority.... If black women were depicted as sexual savages, hot pussies on the lookout for ready prey, then these stereotypes were countered by images of virtuous repressed black ladyhood." Thomas's intervention is rooted in Black feminist thought of the 1960s and 1970s. She presents this iconography as a mirror that makes autonomous agency possible only through glimpses of sisterhood that refuses to centre what hooks and others have called "white racist aesthetics." That is, Thomas's sisterhood breaks from an aesthetic that has privileged not only the way white men look at Black women, but also the gazes of Black men and white feminists over the way Black women see themselves.[12]

In *Ms. Celie's Blues* (2016) (pages 48–49), Thomas reimagines in mirrored acrylic a scene from Steven Spielberg's 1985 film adaptation of Alice Walker's 1982 novel, *The Color Purple*. In it, Celie's eyes are fixed on Shug Avery as Shug sings to her at the club. "The room parts because Shug is focused on [Celie] and she is saying, basically, 'You are everything,'" Thomas explains. "For me, that moment goes toward philosophies like [Jacques] Lacan's notions of beauty, which basically says we don't necessarily see ourselves until we look into a mirror; we can be those mirrors when we see ourselves in each other and have a sense of validation."[13]

The mirror of sisterhood, delighting in female beauty and gender play, bounds each and every muse and icon, friend and lover that Thomas has recorded and collaged, photographed and painted. (This reflection is exemplified by the video installation *Me as Muse* (2016) (page 4), in which the artist makes herself a "mirror image" for her fellow sisters, transforming herself into a modern Venus in repose as the camera moves up her bare body, mapping it.) Speaking about her reinterpretation of *The Color Purple,* she outlines how sisterhood has been a dominant concern in her work: "All of these women oscillate at various moments in their lives, believing or not believing that they are worthy, smart, or beautiful. The truth is developed through their sisterhood relationships as they become mirror images of each other, allowing one another to fully see themselves in order to embody the strength of self to celebrate life and beauty."[14]

Mirroring also surfaces in Thomas's habit of making sisterhood the province of real-life divas: her late mother, Sandra Bush; her partner and constant muse, Racquel Chevremont; the celebrity figures of Oprah, Diana Ross, and Whoopi Goldberg; and former secretary of state Condoleezza Rice, among others. In Thomas's art, they have all appeared visually heroic, sexy, in control of real desire—modelling sisterhood as behaviour. The message: Black women belong to themselves and each other, despite what the images of the broader world would have us believe.

In the four-channel video *Angelitos Negros* (2016) (page 105), in found footage against a white backdrop, Eartha Kitt sings—no, pleads—with painters to fill a stained-glass church with a different celestial reflection: Black angels. She coos: "How come you don't paint our skin if you put love in your art?... Painters, paint me some Black angels now!"[15]

And because Thomas does paint with love, power, and a sense of sisterhood, she has taken the star's plea to heart. "Eartha Kitt is passionately singing and speaking about the lack of positive Black images in the world," Thomas explains. "I was sort of like, 'This song is everything!' It's so timely and it says everything that I am trying to say. I'm putting these Black angels out there—I'm doing it."[16] In just about every medium Thomas has made Black angels, as women who love other women, for display in museums—churches by another name.

Thomas's work concerns sisterhood as existing broadly on a continuum beyond consanguinity and beyond established clichés that simply claim traditional heteronormative constructions of beauty, femininity, power, and desire as embodied neatly in one body or as one dream. Perhaps she has realized, like her sister before her, the Black feminist icon and poet Audre Lorde, that "deep, deep, deep down I know that dream was never mine. And I wept and I cried and I fought and I stormed, but I just knew it. I was Black. I was female. And I was out—*out*—by any construct wherever the power lay."[17] But unlike Lorde, Thomas knew her sisters were dreaming about her and so she dreamed about them. How they could love and learn from each other. How they could meet their own demands. How they could show each other the hallmarks of sisterhood, beauty and power and home.

Antwaun Sargent is a writer and critic based in New York City. He has written for the *New Yorker*, *The Nation*, the *New York Times*, and *Vice*.

**1** Greg Tate, "All the Things You Could Be by Now If James Brown Was a Feminist," in *FlyBoy 2: The Greg Tate Reader* (Durham, NC: Duke University Press, 2016), 187.

**2** Morgan Parker, "Venus Hottentot," *Paris Review*, no. 216 (spring 2016), https://www.theparisreview.org/poetry/6446/hottentot-venus-morgan-parker.

**3** Antwaun Sargent, "Mickalene Thomas on Muses, Models and Mentors," *Interview*, Mar. 9, 2016, https://www.interviewmagazine.com/art/mickalene-thomas.

**4** Elizabeth Alexander, "Toward the Black Interior," in *The Black Interior* (Minneapolis: Graywolf Press, 2004), 9–11.

**5** Ibid.

**6** Denise Murrell, "The Anterior as Muse: Recent Paintings by Mickalene Thomas," in *Mickalene Thomas: Origin of the Universe*, ed. Lisa Melandri (Santa Monica, CA: Santa Monica Museum of Art, 2012), 24.

**7** Robin Coste Lewis, "Voyage of the Sable Venus," in *Voyage of the Sable Venus* (New York: Alfred A. Knopf, 2015), 57–58.

**8** Mickalene Thomas in an interview with Lisa Melandri, "Points of Origin," in *Mickalene Thomas: Origin of the Universe*, ed. Lisa Melandri (Santa Monica: Santa Monica Museum of Art, 2012), 37–38.

**9** Ibid.

**10** bell hooks, "Sisterhood: Political Solidarity Between Women," *Feminist Review*, no. 23, *Socialist-Feminism: Out of the Blue* (summer 1986): 125–38.

**11** Mickalene Thomas, quoted in "Mickalene Thomas: Mentors, Muses, and Celebrities," gallery guide, Contemporary Art Museum Saint Louis, https://camstl.org/wp-content/uploads/2017/12/gallery-guide-mickalene-thomas.pdf, 1–2.

**12** bell hooks, "Feminism Inside: Toward a Black Body Politic," in *Black Male: Representations of Masculinity in Contemporary American Art* (New York: Whitney Museum of American Art, 1995), 127–28.

**13** Sargent, "Mickalene Thomas on Muses, Models, and Mentors."

**14** Thomas, "Mentors, Muses, and Celebrities," 2.

**15** Eartha Kitt, "Paint Me Black Angels" ("Angelitos Negros") from *Sentimental Eartha* (1970).

**16** Thomas, "Mentors, Muses, and Celebrities," 2.

**17** Audre Lorde, in "Revolutionary Hope: A Conversation Between James Baldwin and Audre Lorde," *Essence* (December 1984), 72–73.

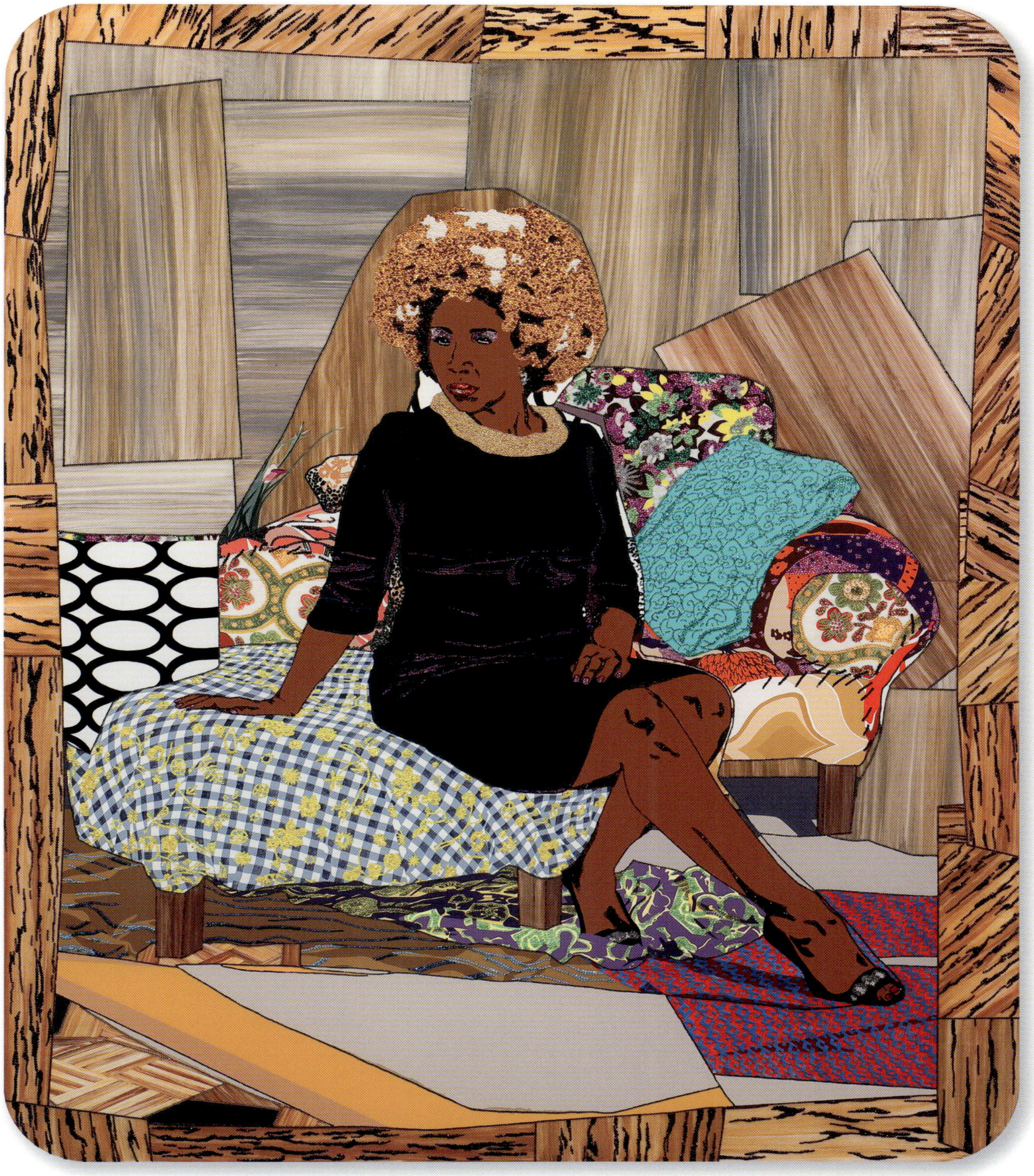

I LEARNED THE HARD WAY, 2010

# *Formation*
## Carla Williams

"Okay, ladies, now let's get in formation...." It was a clarion call from a contemporary queen, a loud 'n' proud shout heard 'round the diaspora. For us. By us. An unequivocal, highly visible work of art celebrating us. A self-affirmation of Black girl magic. True to form, we heard and assembled, in radical alignment. It was time.

The verity and intimacy of the snapshot photograph, created in the moment, was once meant only for the nearest and dearest to ever see. Fifty, sixty, even eighty years ago, when many of these images were made, the subjects could have never conceived of the delight strangers would take in their posing dynamics, in the posturing interplay of friends and family for the camera, the insight and knowledge that their self-representation continues to impart in this contemporary moment.

Carla Williams is an artist and writer based in San Francisco. Her work as a photographer and historian addresses subjects such as identity, family relationships and memory, race and acts of naming, and ideals of beauty.

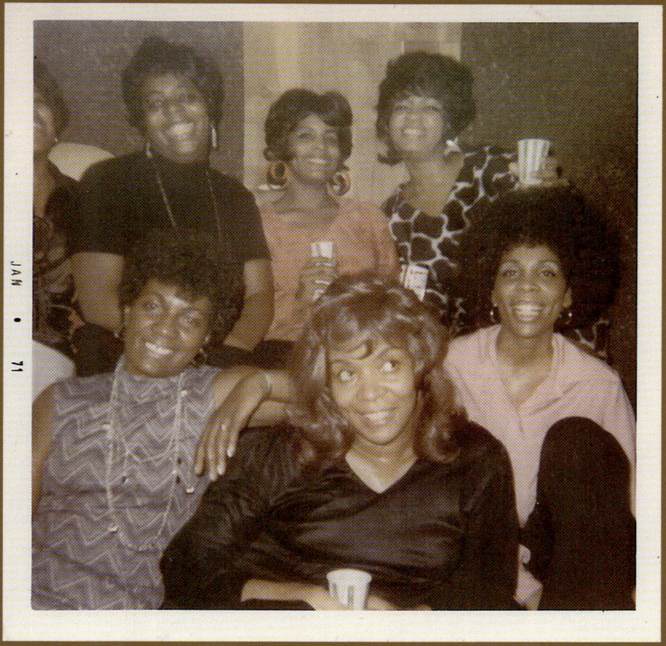
JAN • 71

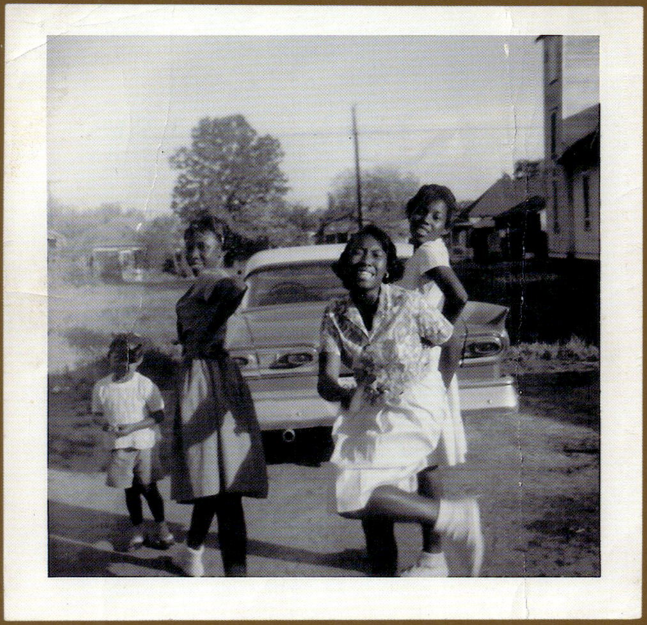

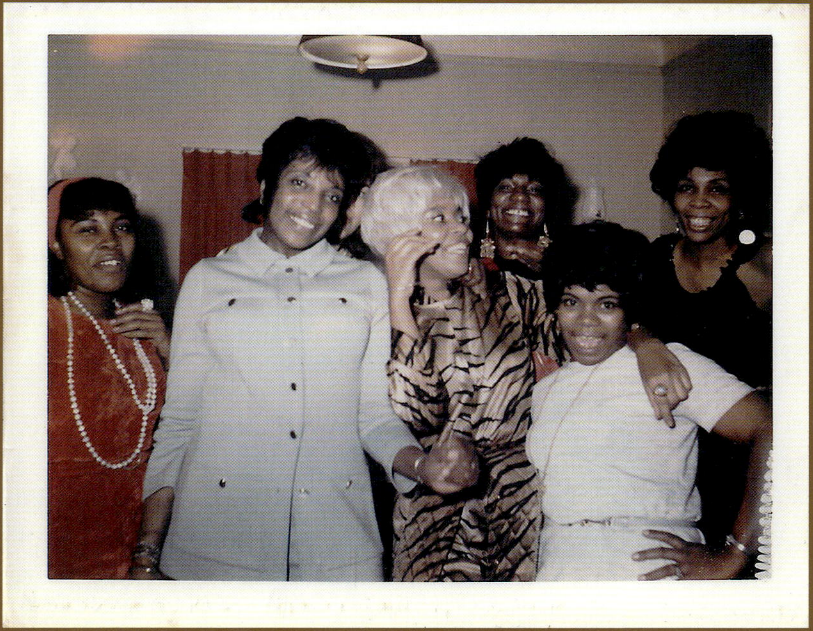

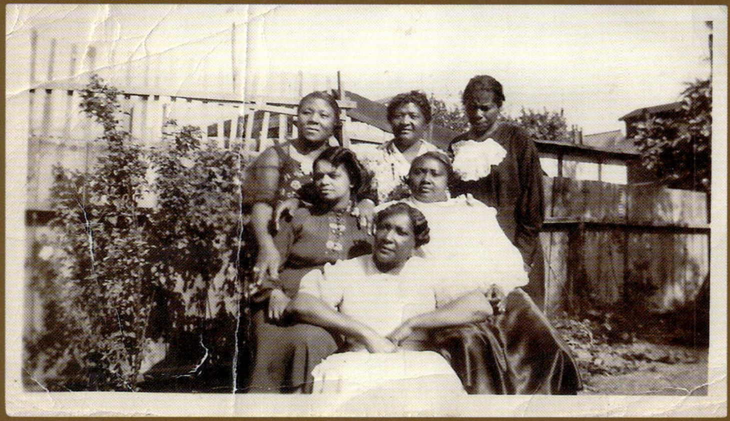

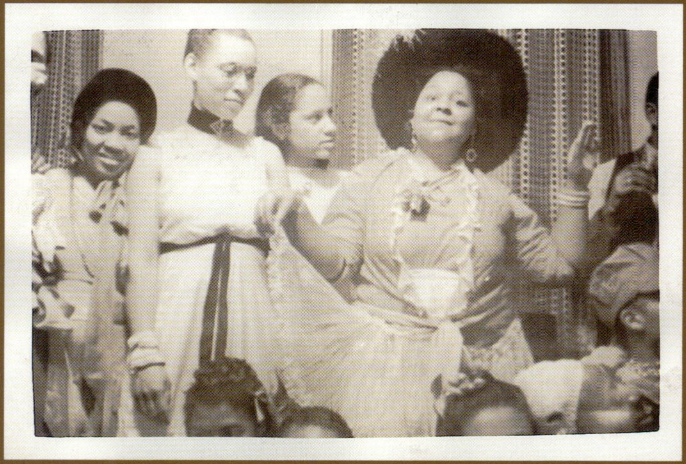

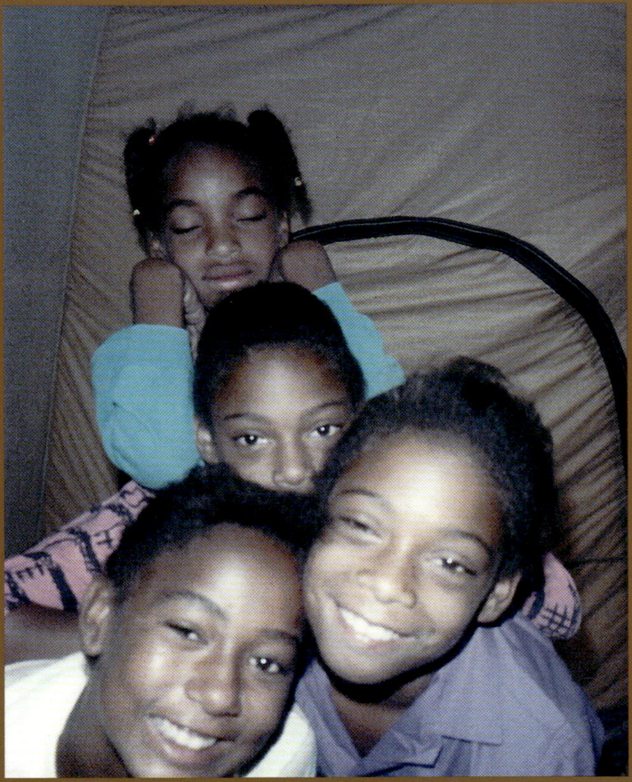
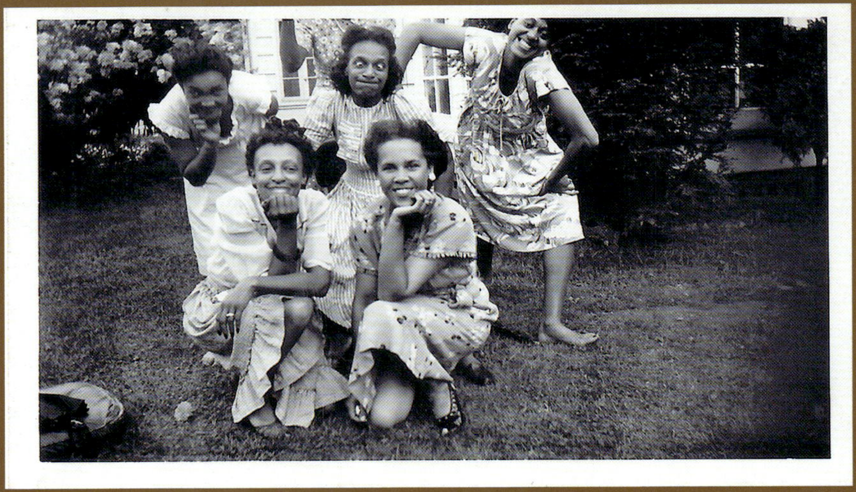
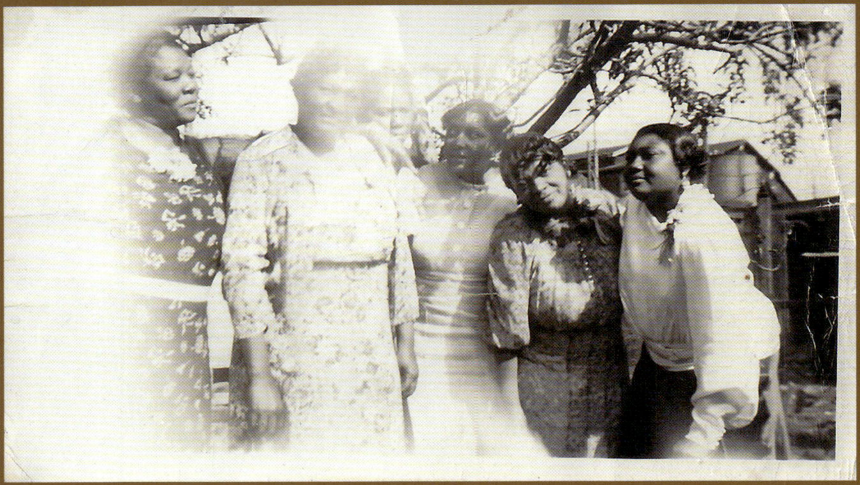
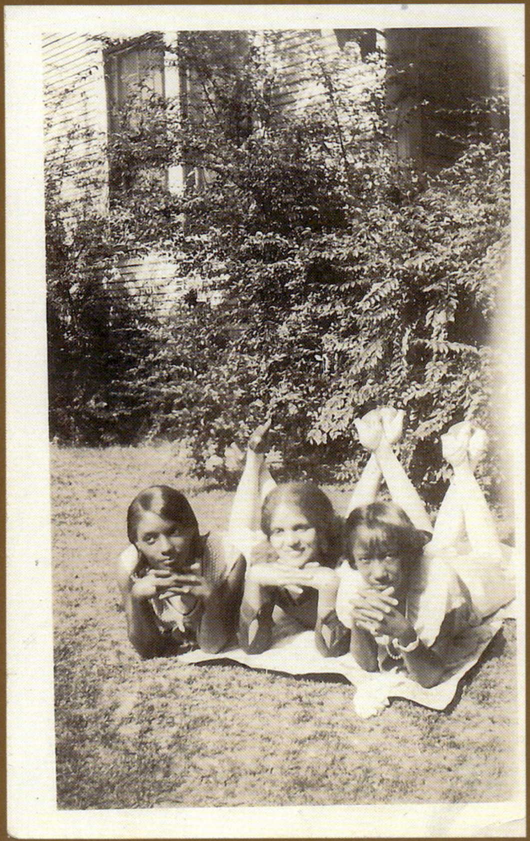
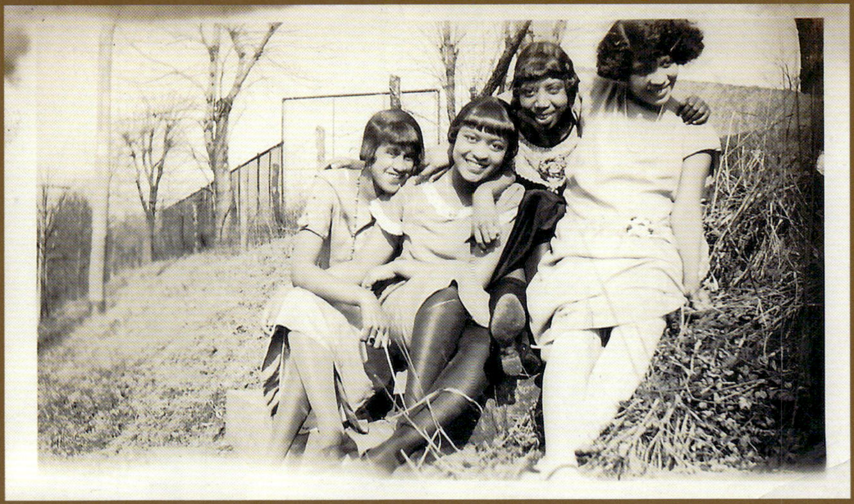

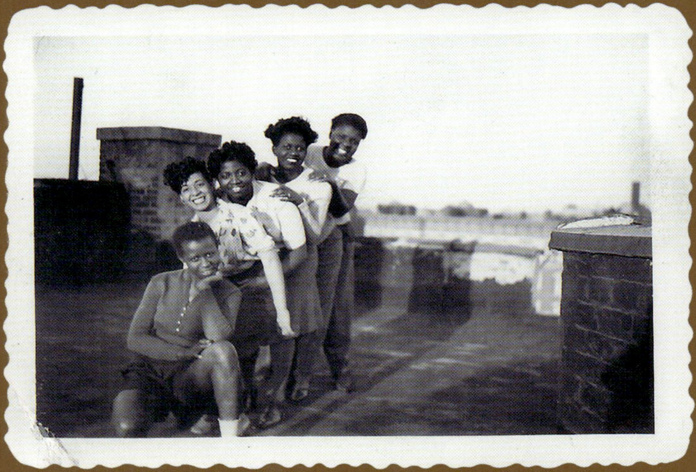

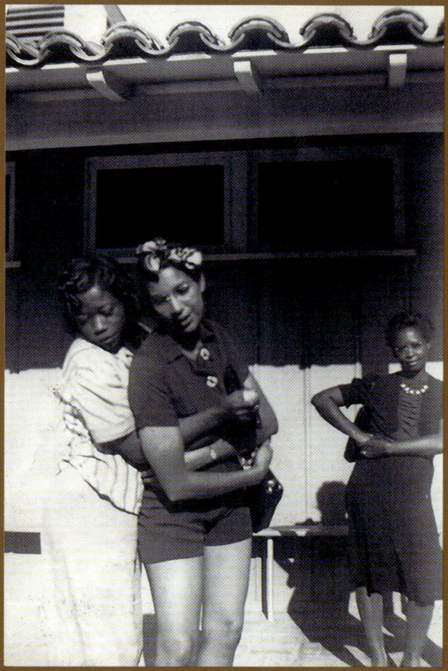

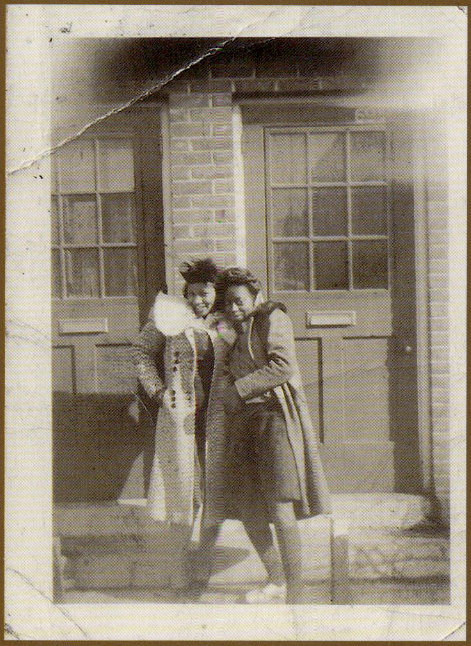

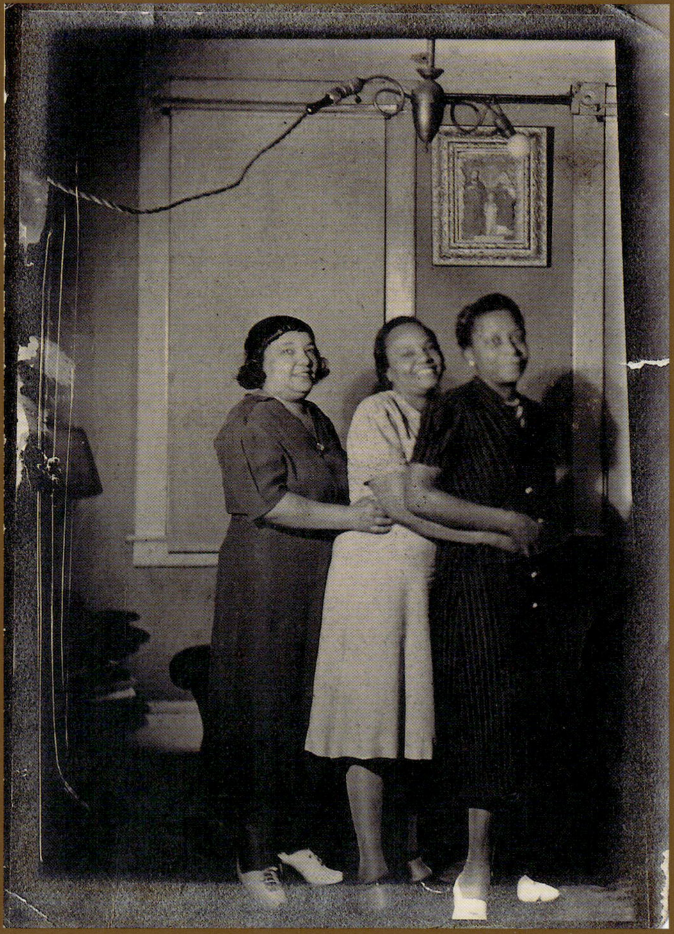

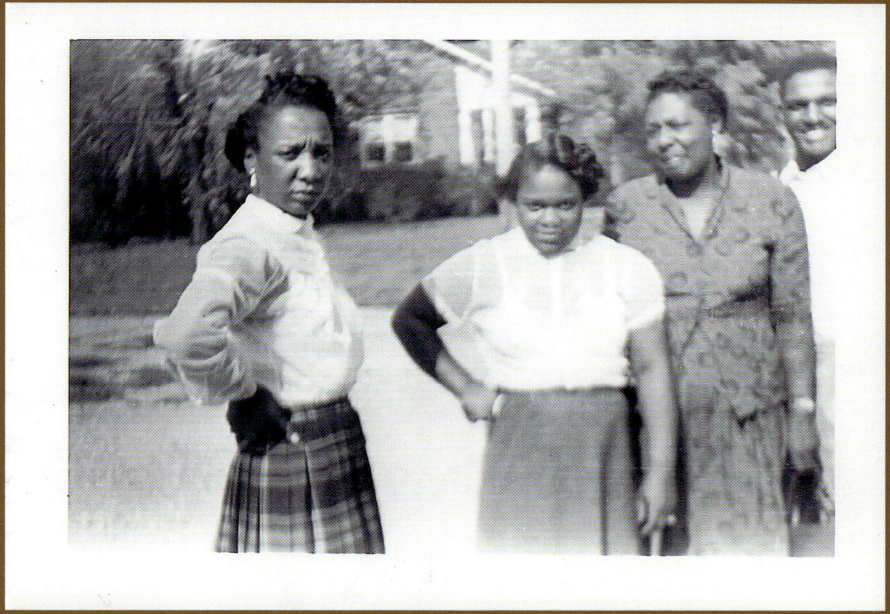

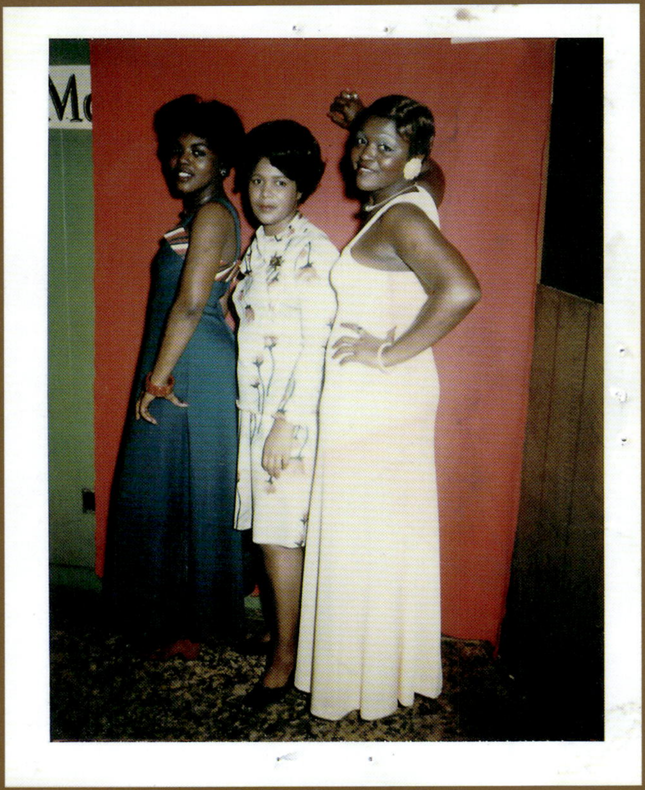

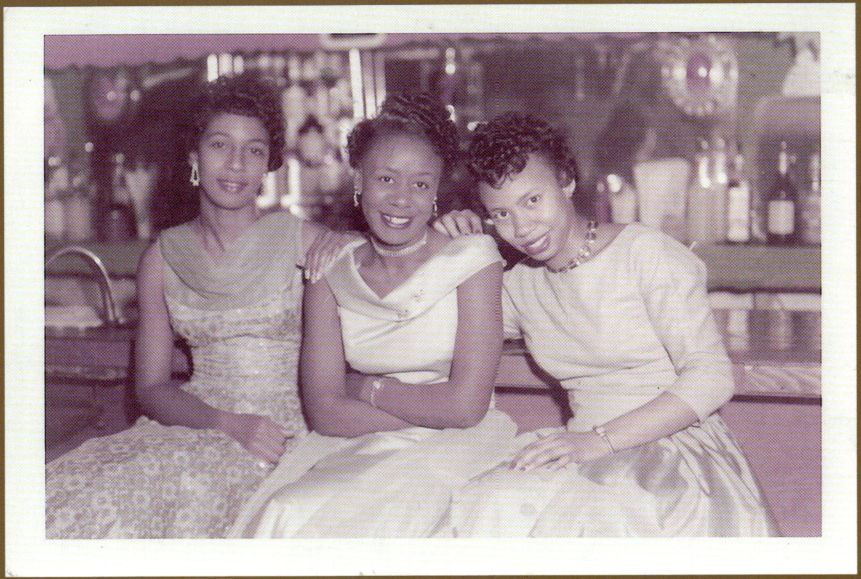

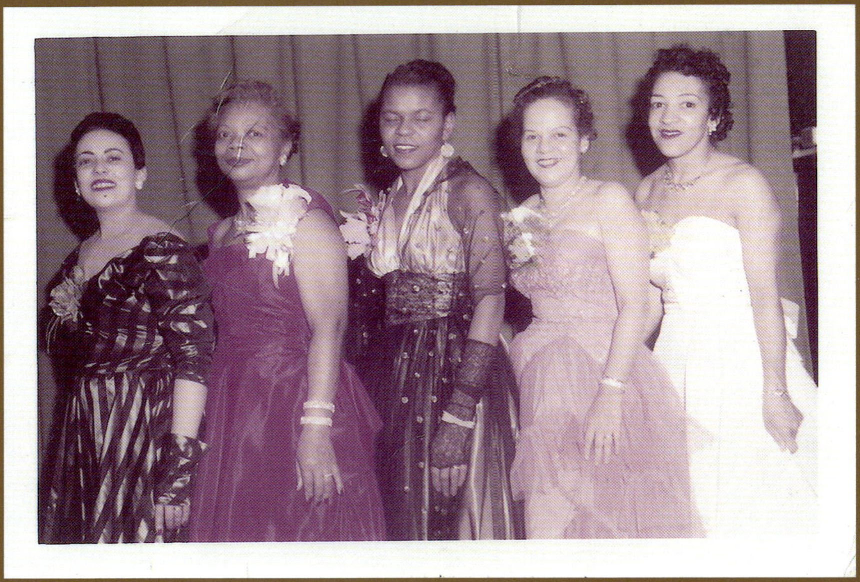

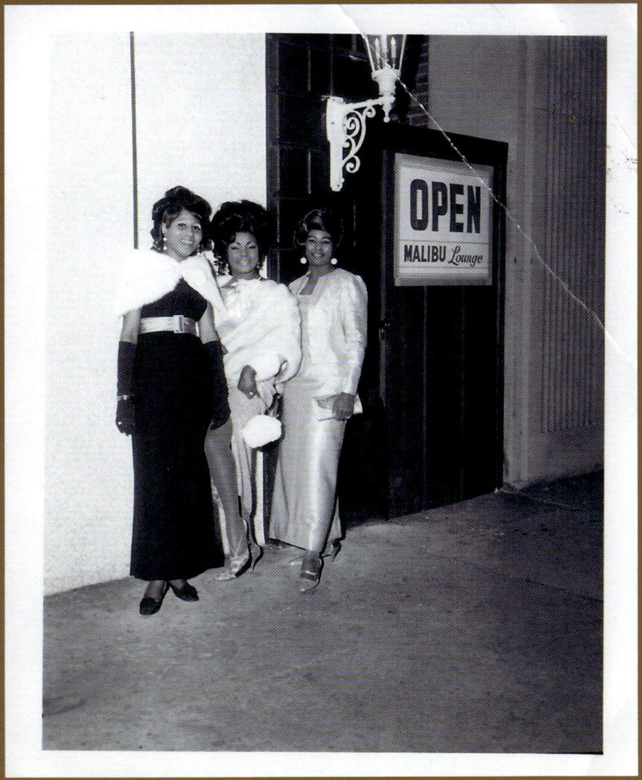
OPEN
MALIBU Lounge

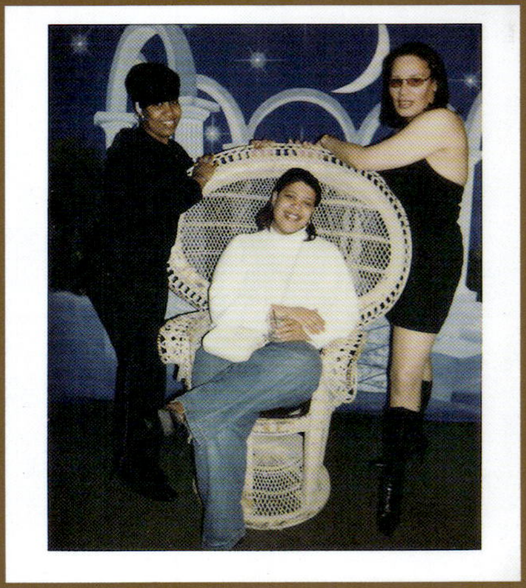

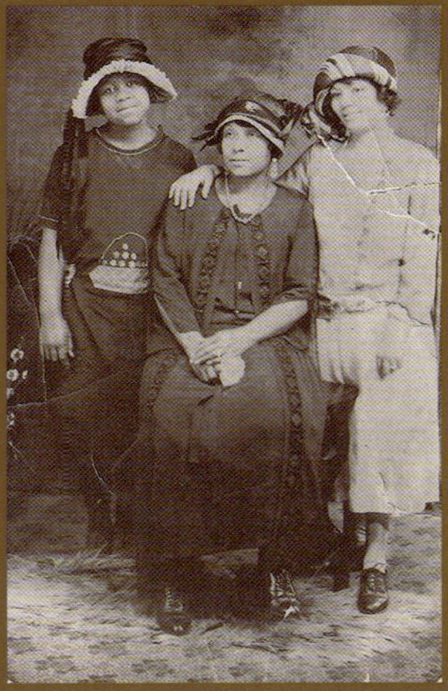

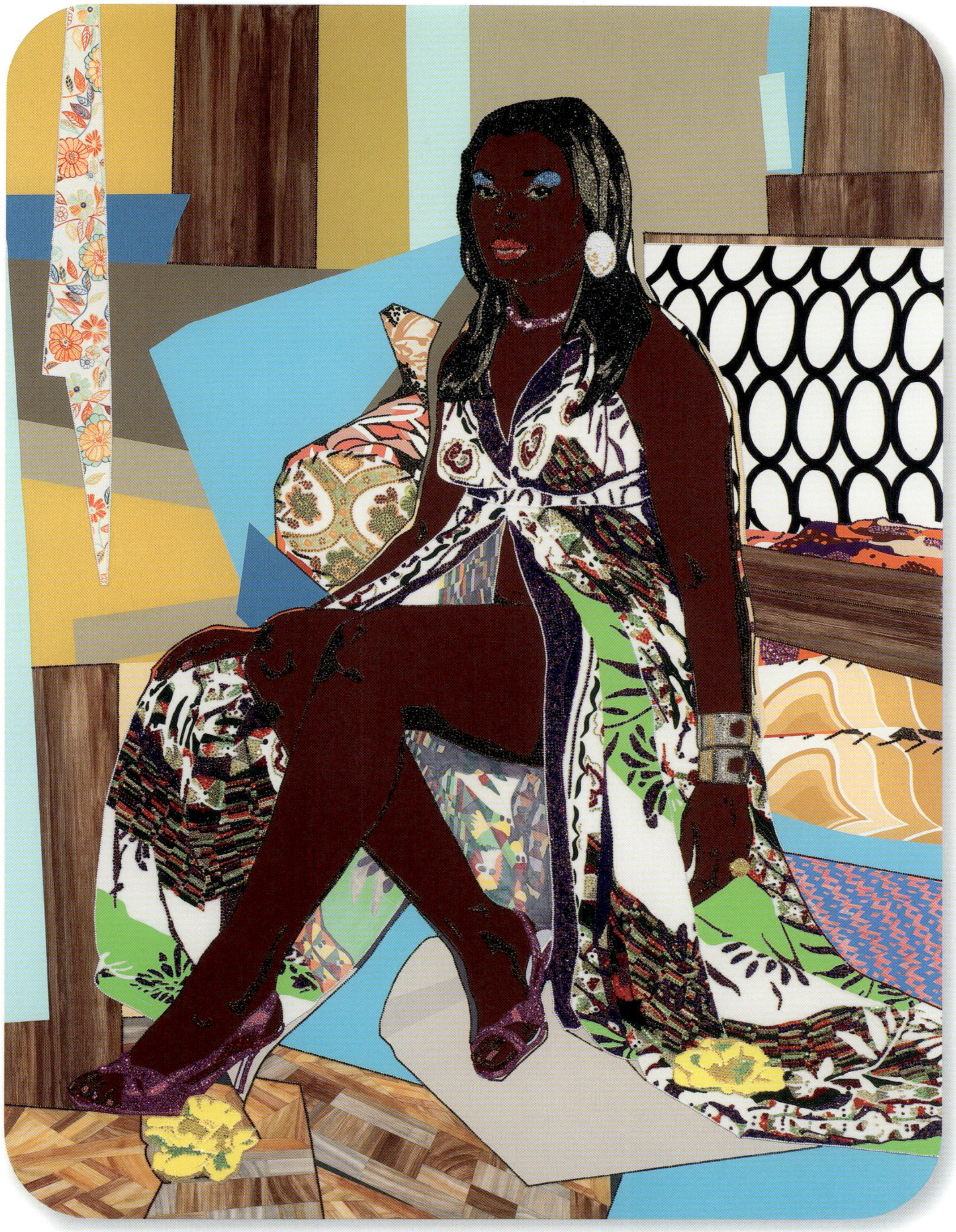

LOVE'S BEEN GOOD TO ME #3, 2010

# *Man Royals and Sodomites: Some Thoughts on the Invisibility of Afro-Caribbean Lesbians* (1991)
# Makeda Silvera

> *This piece was first published in 1988. At that time, to my knowledge, it was difficult for Black women, particularly Caribbean Black women, to "come out" as lesbians in print. I was invited to write this piece for a small publication called* Sight Specific: Lesbians and Representation.
>
> *I remember pondering where to begin: I had no writerly Caribbean role models to call on. I had to search my own oral history in creative ways to write and share this piece. It was both an exciting and a scary time. Over the years it has been reprinted too many times to count—a testimony to the power of oral history, and to the power of vivid storytelling.*
> —Makeda Silvera, September 2018

I will begin with some personal images and voices about woman-loving. These have provided a ground for my search for cultural reflections on my identity as a Black woman artist within the Afro-Caribbean community in Toronto. Although I focus here on my own experience (specifically, Jamaican), I am aware of similarities with the experience of other Third World women of colour whose history and culture has been subjected to colonisation and imperialism.

I spent the first thirteen years of my life in Jamaica among strong women. My great-grandmother, my grandmother and grant-aunts were major influences in my life. There are also men whom I remember with fondness—my grandmother's "man friend" G., my Uncle Bertie, his friend Paul, Mr. Minott, Uncle B. and Uncle Freddy. And there were men like Mr. Eden who terrified me because of stories about his "walking" fingers and his liking for girls under age fourteen.

I lived in a four-bedroom house with my grandmother, Uncle Bertie and two female tenants. On the same piece of land, my grandmother had other tenants, mostly women and lots of children. The big verandah of our house played a vital role in the social life of this community. It was on the verandah that I received my first education on "Black women's strength"—not only from their strength, but also from the daily humiliations they bore at work and in relationships. European experience coined the term "feminism," but the term "Black women's strength" reaches beyond Eurocentric definitions to describe what is the cultural continuity of my own struggles.

The verandah. My grandmother sat on the verandah in the evenings after all the chores were done to read the newspaper. People—mostly women—gathered there to discuss "life." Life covered every conceivable topic—economic, local, political, social and sexual: the high price of salt-fish, the scarcity of flour, the nice piece of yellow yam bought at Coronation market, Mr. Lam, the shopkeeper who was taking "liberty" with Miss Inez, the fights women had with their menfolk, work, suspicions of Miss Iris and Punsie carrying on something between them, the cost of school books....

My grandmother usually had lots of advice to pass on to the women of the verandah, all grounded in the Bible. Granny believed in Jesus, in good and evil and in repentance. She was also a practical and sociable woman. Her faith didn't interfere with her perception of what it meant to be a poor Black woman; neither did it interfere with our Friday night visits to my Aunt Marie's bar. I remember sitting outside on the piazza with my grandmother, two grand-aunts and three or four of their women friends. I liked their flashy smiles and I was fascinated by their independence, ease and their laughter. I loved their names—Cherry Rose, Blossom, Jonesie, Poinsietta, Ivory, Pearl, Iris, Bloom, Dahlia, Babes. Whenever the conversation came around to some "big 'oman talk"—who was sleeping with whom or whose daughter just got "fallen"—I was sent off to get a glass of water for an adult, or a bottle of Kola champagne. Every Friday night I drank as much as half a dozen bottles of Kola champagne, but I still managed to hear snippets of words, tail ends of conversations about women together.

In Jamaica, the words used to describe many of these women would be "Man Royal" and/or "Sodomite." Dread words. So dread that women dare not use these words to name themselves. They were names given to women by men to describe aspects of our lives that men neither understood nor approved.

I heard "sodomite" whispered a lot during my primary school years, and tales of women secretly having sex, joining at the genitals, and being taken to the hospital to be "cut" apart were told in the schoolyard. Invariably, one of the women would die. Every five to ten years the same story would surface. At times, it would even be published in the newspapers. Such stories always generated much talking and speculation from "Bwoy dem kinda gal naasti sah!" to some wise old woman saying, "But dis caan happen, after two shutpan caan join"—meaning identical objects cannot go into the other. The act of loving someone of the same sex was sinful, abnormal—something to hide. Even today, it isn't unusual or uncommon to be asked, "So how do two 'omen do it?... What unnu use for a penis?... Who is the man and who is the 'oman?" It's inconceivable that women can have intimate relationships that are whole, that are not lacking because of the absence of a man. It's assumed that women in such relationships must be imitating men.

The word "sodomite" derives from the Old Testament. Its common use to describe lesbians (or any strong independent woman) is peculiar to Jamaica—a culture historically and strongly grounded in the Bible. Although Christian values have dominated the world, their effect in slave colonies is particular. Our foreparents gained access to literacy through the Bible when they were being indoctrinated by missionaries. It provided powerful and ancient stories of strength, endurance and hope which reflected their own fight against oppression. This book has been so powerful that it continues to bind our lives with its racism and misogyny. Thus, the importance the Bible plays in Afro-Caribbean culture must be recognized in order to understand the historical and political context for the invisibility of lesbians. The wrath of God "rained down burning sulphur on Sodom and Gomorrah" (Genesis 19:23). How could a Caribbean woman claim the name?

When, thousands of miles away and fifteen years after my school days, my grandmother was confronted with my love for a woman, her reaction was determined by her Christian faith and by this dread word sodomite—its meaning, its implication, its history.

And when, Bible in hand, my grandmother responded to my love by sitting me down, at the age of twenty-seven, to quote Genesis, it was within the context of this tradition, this politic. When she pointed out that "this was a white people ting," or "a ting only people with mixed blood was involved in" (to explain or include my love with a woman of mixed race), it was strong denial of many ordinary Black working-class women she knew.

It was finally through my conversations with my grandmother, my mother and my mother's friend five years later that I began to realize the scope of this denial which was intended to dissuade and protect me. She knew too well that any woman who took a woman lover was attempting to walk on fire—entering a "no man's land." I began to see how commonplace the act of loving women really was, particularly in working-class communities. I realized, too, just how heavily shame and silence weighed down this act.

*A conversation with a friend of my mother:*

Well, when I growing up we didn't hear much 'bout woman and woman. They weren't "suspect." There was much more talk about "batty man business" when I was a teenager in the 1950s.

I remember one story about a man who was "suspect" and that every night when he was coming home, a group of guys use to lay wait him and stone him so viciously that he had to run for his life. Dem time, he was safe only in the day.

Now with women, nobody really suspected. I grew up in the country and I grew up seeing women holding hands, hugging up, sleeping together in one bed and there was no question. Some of this was based purely on emotional friendship but I also knew of cases where the women were dealing but no one really suspected. Close people around knew, but not everyone. It wasn't a thing that you would go out and broadcast. It would be something just between the two people.

Also one important thing is that the women who were involved carried on with life just the same, no big political statements were made. These women still went to church, still got baptised, still went on pilgrimage, and I am thinking about one particular woman name Aunt Vie, a very strong woman, a strong-willed and everything, they use to call her "man-royal" behind her back, but no one ever dare to meddle with her.

Things are different now in Jamaica. Now all you have to do is not respond to a man's call to you and dem call you sodomite or lesbian. I guess it was different back then forty years ago because it was harder for anybody to really conceive of two woman sleeping and being sexual. But I do remember when you were "suspect," people would talk about you. You were definitely classed as "different," "not normal," a bit "crazy." But women never really got stoned like the men.

What I remember is that if you were a single woman alone or two single women living together and a few people suspected this...and when I say a few people I mean like a few guys, sometimes other crimes were committed against the women. Some very violent, some very subtle. Battery was common, especially in Kingston. A group of men would suspect a woman or have it out for her because she was a "sodomite" or because she act "man-royal" and so the men would organise and gang rape whichever woman was "suspect." Sometimes it was reported in the newspapers, other times it wasn't—but when you live in a little community, you don't need a newspaper to tell you what's going on. You know by word of mouth and those stories were frequent. Sometimes you also knew the men who did the battery.

Other subtle forms of this was "scorning" the women. Meaning that you didn't eat anything from them, especially a cooked meal. It was almost as if those accused for being "man-royal" or "sodomite" could contaminate.

*A conversation with my grandmother:*

I am only telling you this so that you can understand that this is not a profession to be proud of and to get involved in. Everybody should be curious and I know you born with that, ever since you growing up as a child and I can't fight against that, because that is how everybody get to know what's in the world. I am only telling you this because when you were a teenager, you always say you want to experience everything and make up your mind on your own. You didn't like people telling you what was wrong and right. That always use to scare me.

Experience is good, yes. But it have to be balanced, you have to know when you have too much experience in one area. I am telling you this because I think you have enough experience in this to decide now to go back to the normal way. You have two children. Do you want them to grow up knowing this is the life you have taken? But this is for you to decide....

Yes, there was a lot of women involved with women in Jamaica. I knew a lot of them when I was growing up in the country in the 1920s. I didn't really associate with them. Mind you, I was not rude to them. My mother wouldn't stand for any rudeness from any of her children to adults.

I remember a woman we use to call Miss Bibi. She live next to us—her husband was a fisherman, I think he drowned before I was born. She had a little wooden house that back onto the sea, the same as our house. She was quiet, always reading. That I remember about her because she use to go to the little public library at least four days out of the week. And she could talk. Anything you want to know, just ask Miss Bibi and she could tell you. She was a mulatto woman, but poor. Anytime I had any school work that I didn't understand, I use to ask her. The one thing I remember though, we wasn't allowed in her house by my mother, so I use to talk to her outside, but she didn't seem to mind that. Some people use to think she was mad because spent so much time alone. But I didn't think that because anything she helped me with, I got a good mark on it in school.

She was colourful in her own way, but quiet, always alone, except when her friend come and visit her once a year for two weeks. Them times I didn't see Miss Bibi much because my mother told me I couldn't go and visit her. Sometimes I would see her in the market exchanging and bartering fresh fish for vegetables and fruits. I use to see her friend too. She was a jet-Black woman, always had her hair tied in bright coloured cloth and she always had on big gold earrings. People used to say she live on the other side of the island with her husband and children and she came to Port Maria once a year to visit Miss Bibi.

My mother and father were great storytellers and I learnt that from them, but is from Miss Bibi that I think I learnt to love reading so much as a child. It wasn't until I move to Kingston that I notice other women like Miss Bibi....

Let me tell you about Jones. Do you remember her? Well she was the woman who live the next yard over from us. She is the one who really turn me against people like that, why I fear so much for you to be involved in this ting. She was very loud. Very show-off. Always dressed in pants and man-shirt that she borrowed from her husband. Sometimes she use to invite me over to her house, but I didn't go. She always had her hair in a bob hair cut, always barefoot and tending to her garden and her fruit trees. She tried to get me involved in that kind of life but I said no. At the time I remember I needed some money to borrow and she lent me, later she told me I didn't have to pay her back, but to come over to her house and see the thing she had that was sweeter than what any man could offer me. I told her no and eventually paid her back the money.

We still continued to talk. It was hard not to like Jonesie—that's what everybody called her. She was open and easy to talk to. But still there was a fear in me about her. To me it seem like she was in a dead end with nowhere to go. I don't want that for you.

I left my grandmother's house that day feeling anger and sadness for Miss Jones—maybe for myself, who knows. I was feeling boxed in. I had said nothing. I'd only listened quietly.

In bed that night, I thought about Miss Jones. I cried for her (for me) silently. I remember her, a mannish looking Indian woman, with flashy gold teeth, a Craven A cigarette always between them. She was always nice to me as a child. She had the sweetest, juiciest Julie, Bombay, and East Indian mangoes on the street. She always gave me mangoes over the fence. I remember the dogs in her yard and the sign on her gate "Beware of bad dogs." I never went into her house, though I was always curious.

I vaguely remember her pants and shirts, though I never thought anything of them until my grandmother pointed them out. Neither did I recall that dreaded word being used to describe her, although everyone on the street knew about her.

*A conversation with my mother:*

Yes I remember Miss Jones. She smoke a lot, drank a lot. In fact, she was an alcoholic. When I was in my teens she use to come over to our house—always on the verandah. I can't remember her sitting down—seems she was always standing up, smoking, drinking and reminiscing. She constantly talked about the past, about her life and it was always on the verandah. And it was always women: young women she knew when she was a young woman, the fun they had together and how good she would make love to a woman. She would say to whoever was listening on the verandah, "Dem girls I use to have sex with was shapely. You shoulda know me when I was younger, pretty and shapely just like the 'oman dem I use to have as my 'oman."

People use to tease her on the street, but not about being a lesbian or calling her sodomite. People use to tease her when she was drunk, because she would leave the rumshop and stagger down the avenue to her house.

I remember the women she use to carry home, usually in the daytime. A lot of women from downtown, higglers and fishwomen. She use to boast about knowing all kinds of women from Coronation market and her familiarity with them. She had a husband who lived with her and that served as her greatest protection against other men taking steps with her. Not that anybody could easily take advantage of Miss Jones, she could stand up for herself. But having a husband did help. He was a very quiet, insular man. He didn't talk to anyone on the street. He had no friends so it wasn't easy for anyone to come up to him and gossip about his wife.

No one could go to her house without being invited, but I wouldn't say she was a private person. She was a loner. She went to the rumshops alone, she drank alone, she staggered home alone. The only time I ever saw her with somebody were the times when she went off to the Coronation market or some other place downtown to find a woman and bring her home. The only times I remember her engaging in conversation with anybody was when she came over on the verandah to talk about her women and what they did in bed. That was all she let out about herself. There was nothing about how she was feeling, whether she was sad or depressed, lonely, happy. Nothing. She seemed to cover up all that with her loudness and her vulgarness and her constant threat—which was all it was—to beat up anybody who troubled her or teased her when she was coming home from the rumshop.

Now Cherry Rose—do you remember her? She was a good friend of Aunt Marie and of Mama's. She was also a sodomite. She was loud too, but different from Miss Jones. She was much more outgoing. She was a barmaid and had lots of friends—both men and women. She also had the kind of personality that attracted people—very vivacious, always laughing, talking and touching. She didn't have any children, but Gem did.

Do you remember Miss Gem? Well she had children and she was also a barmaid. She also had lots of friends. She also had a man friend named Mickey, but that didn't matter because some women had their men and still had women they carried on with. The men usually didn't know what was going on, and seeing as these men just come and go and usually on their own time, they weren't around every day and night.

Miss Pearl was another one that was in that kind of thing. She was a dressmaker, she use to sew really good. Where Gem was light complexion, she was a very black Black woman with deep dimples. Where Gem was a bit plump, Pearl was slim, but with big breast and a big bottom. They were both pretty women.

I don't remember hearing that word sodomite a lot about them. It was whispered sometimes behind their backs, but never in front of them. And they were so alive and talkative that people were always around them.

The one woman I almost forgot was Miss Opal, a very quiet woman. She use to be friends with Miss Olive and was always out at her bar sitting down. I can't remember much about her except she didn't drink like Miss Jones and she wasn't vulgar. She was soft-spoken, a half-Chinese woman. Her mother was born in Hong Kong and her father was a Black man. She could really bake. She use to supply shops with cakes and other pastries.

So there were many of those kind of women around. But it wasn't broadcast.

—

I remember them. Not as lesbians or sodomites or man royals, but as women that I liked. Women who I admired. Strong women, some colourful, some quiet.

I loved Cherry Rose's style. I loved her loudness, the way she challenged men in arguments, the bold way she laughed in their faces, the jingle of her gold bracelets. Her colourful and stylish way of dressing. She was full of wit; words came alive in her mouth.

Miss Gem: I remember her big double iron bed. That was where Paula and Lorraine (her daughters, my own age) and I spent a whole week together when we had chicken pox. My grandmother took me there to stay for the company. It was fun. Miss Gem lived right above her bar and so at any time we could look through the window and onto the piazza and street which was bursting with energy and life. She was a very warm woman, patient and caring. Every day she would make soup for us and tell us stories. Later on in the evening she would bring us Kola champagne.

Miss Pearl sewed dresses for me. She hardly ever used her tape measure—she could just take one look at you and make you a dress fit for a queen. What is she doing now, I asked myself? And Miss Opal, with her calm and quiet, where is she—still baking?

What stories could these lesbians have told us? I, an Afro-Caribbean woman living in Canada, come with this baggage—their silenced stories. My grandmother and mother know the truth, but silence still surrounds us. The truth remains a secret to the rest of the family and friends, and I must decide whether to continue to sew this cloth of denial or break free, creating and becoming the artist that I am, bring alive the voices and images of Cherry Rose, Miss Gem, Miss Jones, Opal, Pearl, and others....

There is more at risk for us than for white women. Through three hundred years of history we have carried memories and the scars of racism and violence with us. We are the sister, the daughter, mothers of a people enslaved by colonialists and imperialists. Under slavery, production and reproduction were inextricably linked. Reproduction served not only to increase the labour force of slave owners but also, by "domesticating" the enslaved, facilitated the process of social conditions by focusing on those aspects of life in which they could express their own desires. Sex was an area in which to articulate one's humanity, but, because it was tied to attempts "to define oneself as human," gender roles, as well as the act of sex, became badges of status. To be male was to be the stud, the procreator; to be female was to be fecund, and one's femininity was measured by the ability to attract and hold a man, and to bear children. In this way, slavery and the post-emancipated colonial order defined the structures of patriarchy and heterosexuality as necessary for social mobility and acceptance.

Socio-economic conditions and the quest for a better life have seen steady migration from Jamaica and the rest of the Caribbean to the U.S., Britain and Canada. Upon my arrival, I became part of the so-called "visible minorities" encompassing Blacks, Asians and Native North Americans in Canada. I live with a legacy of continued racism and prejudice. We confront this daily, both as individuals and as organized political groups. Yet for those of us who are lesbians, there is another struggle: the struggle for acceptance and positive self-definition within our own communities. Too often, we have had to sacrifice our love for women in political meetings that have been dominated by the "we are the world" attitude of heterosexual ideology. We have had to hide too often that part of our identity which contributes profoundly to make up the whole.

Many lesbians have worked, like me, in the struggles of Black people since the 1950s. We have been on marches every time one of us gets murdered by the police. We have been at sit-ins and vigils. We have flyered, postered, we have cooked and baked for the struggle. We have tended to the youths. And we have all at one time or another given support to men in our community, all the time painfully holding onto, obscuring, our secret lives. When we do walk out of the closet (or are thrown out), the "ideologues" of the Black communities say "Yes, she was a radical sistren but, I don't know what happened, she just went the wrong way." What is implicit in this is that one cannot be a lesbian and continue to do political work, and not surprisingly, it follows that a Black lesbian/artist cannot create using the art forms of our culture. For example, when a heterosexual male friend came to my house I put on a dub poetry tape. He asked, "Are you sure that sistren is a lesbian?"

"Why?" I asked.

"Because this poem sounds wicked; it have lots of rhythm, it sounds cultural."

Another time, another man commented on my work, "That book you wrote on domestic workers is really a fine piece of work. I didn't know you were that informed about the economic politics of the Caribbean and Canada." What are we to assume from this? That Afro-Caribbean lesbians have no Caribbean culture? That they lose their community politics when they sleep with women? Or that Afro-Caribbean culture is a heterosexual commodity?

The presence of an "out" Afro-Caribbean lesbian in our community is dealt with by suspicion and fear from both men and our heterosexual Black sisters. It brings into question the assumption of heterosexuality as the only "normal" way. It forces them to acknowledge something that has always been covered up. It forces them to look at women differently and brings into question the traditional Black female role. Negative response from our heterosexual Black sister, though more painful, is, to a certain extent, understandable because we have no race privilege and very, very few of us have class privilege. The one privilege within our group is heterosexual. We have all suffered at the hands of this racist system at one time or another and to many heterosexual Black women it is inconceivable, almost frightening, that one could turn back on credibility in our community and the society at large by being lesbian. These women are also afraid that they will be labelled "lesbian" by association. It is that fear, that homophobia, which keeps Black women isolated.

The Toronto Black community has not dealt with sexism. It has not been pushed to do so. Neither has it given a thought to its heterosexism. In 1988, my grandmother's fear is very real, very alive. One takes a chance when one writes about being an Afro-Caribbean lesbian. There is the fear that one might not live to write more. There is the danger of being physically "disciplined" for speaking as a woman-identified woman.

And what of our white lesbian sisters and their community? They have learnt well from the civil rights movement about organizing, and with race and some class privilege, they have built a predominantly white lesbian (and gay) movement—a pre-condition for a significant body of work by a writer or artist. They have demanded and received recognition from politicians (no matter how little). But this recognition has not been extended to Third World lesbians of colour—neither from politicians nor from white lesbian (and gay) organizations. The white lesbian organizations/groups have barely (some not at all) begun to deal with or acknowledge their own racism, prejudice and biases—all learned from a system which feeds on their ignorance and grows stronger from its instutionalised racism. Too often white women focus only on their oppression as lesbians, ignoring the more complex oppression of non-white women who are also lesbians. We remain outsiders in these groups, without image or political voices that echo our own. We know too clearly that, as non-white lesbians in this country, we are politically and socially at the very bottom of the heap. Denial of such differences robs us of true visibility. We must identify and define these differences, and challenge the movements and groups that are not accessible to non-whites—challenge groups that are not accountable.

But where does this leave us as Afro-Caribbean lesbians, as part of this "visible minority" community? As Afro-Caribbean women we are still at the stage where we have to imagine and discover our existence, past and present. As lesbians, we are even more marginalised, less visible. The absence of a national Black lesbian and gay movement through which to begin to name ourselves is disheartening. We have no political organization to support us and through which we could demand respect from our communities. We need such an organization to represent our interests, both in coalition-building with other lesbian/gay organizations, and in the struggles which shape our future—through which we hope to transform the social, political and economic systems of oppression as they affect all peoples.

Though not yet on a large scale, lesbians and gays of Caribbean descent are beginning to seek each other out—are slowly organizing. Younger lesbians and gays of colour are beginning to challenge and force their parents and Black community to deal with their sexuality. They have formed groups, "Zami for Black and Caribbean gays and lesbians" and "Lesbians of Colour," to name two.

The need to make connections with other Caribbean and Third World people of colour who are lesbian and gay is urgent. This is where we can begin to build that other half of our community, to create wholeness through our art. This is where we will find the support and strength to struggle, to share our histories and to record these histories in books, documentaries, film, sound, and art. We will create a rhythm that is uniquely ours—proud, powerful and gay, naming ourselves, and taking our space within the larger history of Afro-Caribbean peoples.

—

**REPRINTED FROM *PIECE OF MY HEART: A LESBIAN OF COLOUR ANTHOLOGY*, ED. MAKEDA SILVERA (TORONTO: SISTER VISION PRESS, 1991), 14–26.**

Makeda Silvera is a Jamaican-born writer who has made Canada her home for most of her life. She broke new ground in the 1980s as a Black feminist lesbian activist when she co-founded Sister Vision: Black Women and Women of Colour Press. Her previous publications include the novel *The Heart Does Not Bend*; two short-story collections (*Remembering G* and *Her Head a Village*); *Growing Up Black*, a guide for youth; and *Silenced*, a compendium of oral histories by Caribbean domestic workers. She also edited *The Other Woman: Women of Colour in Contemporary Canadian Literature* and *Piece of My Heart: A Lesbian of Colour Anthology*.

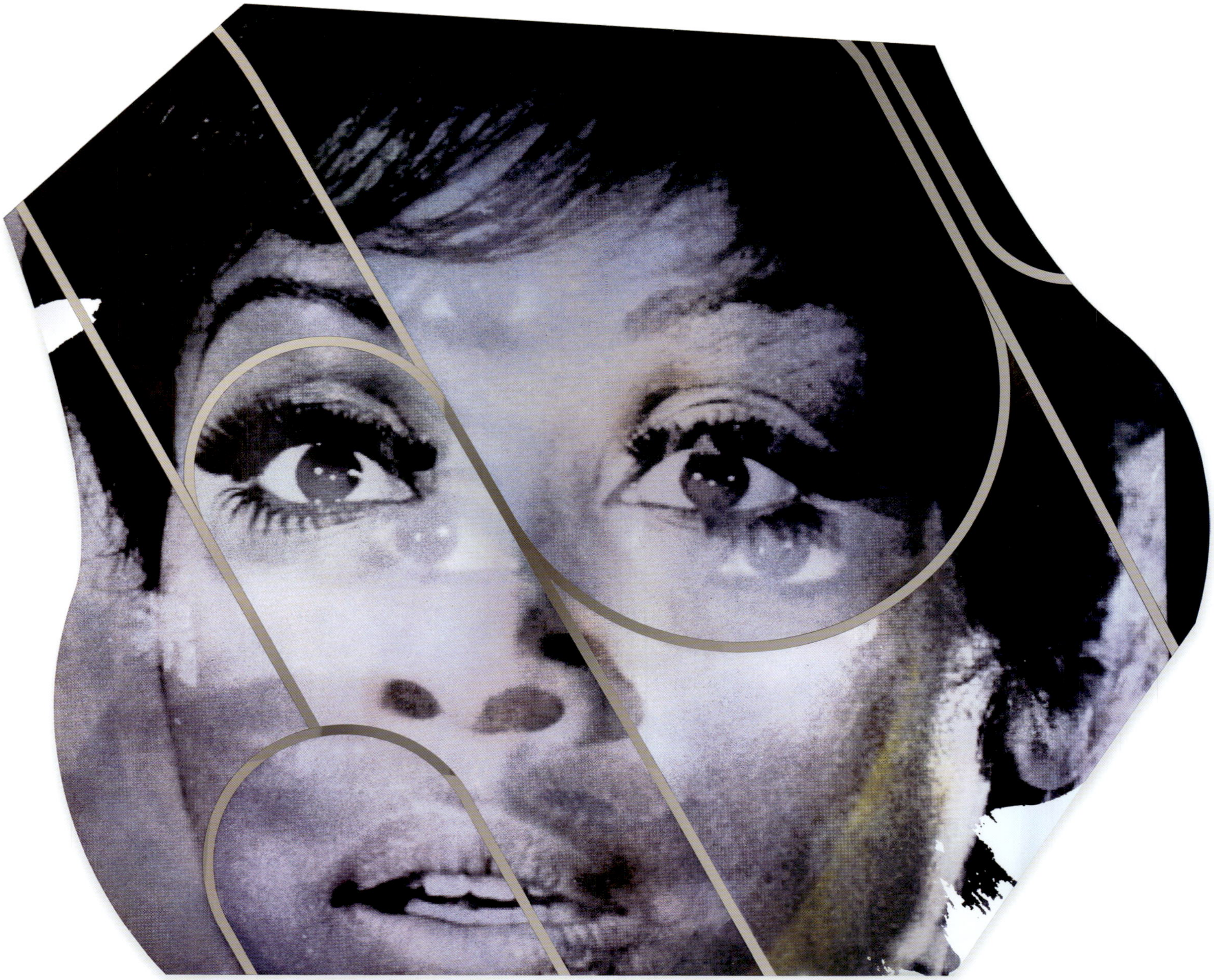

DIAHANN CARROLL #2, 2017

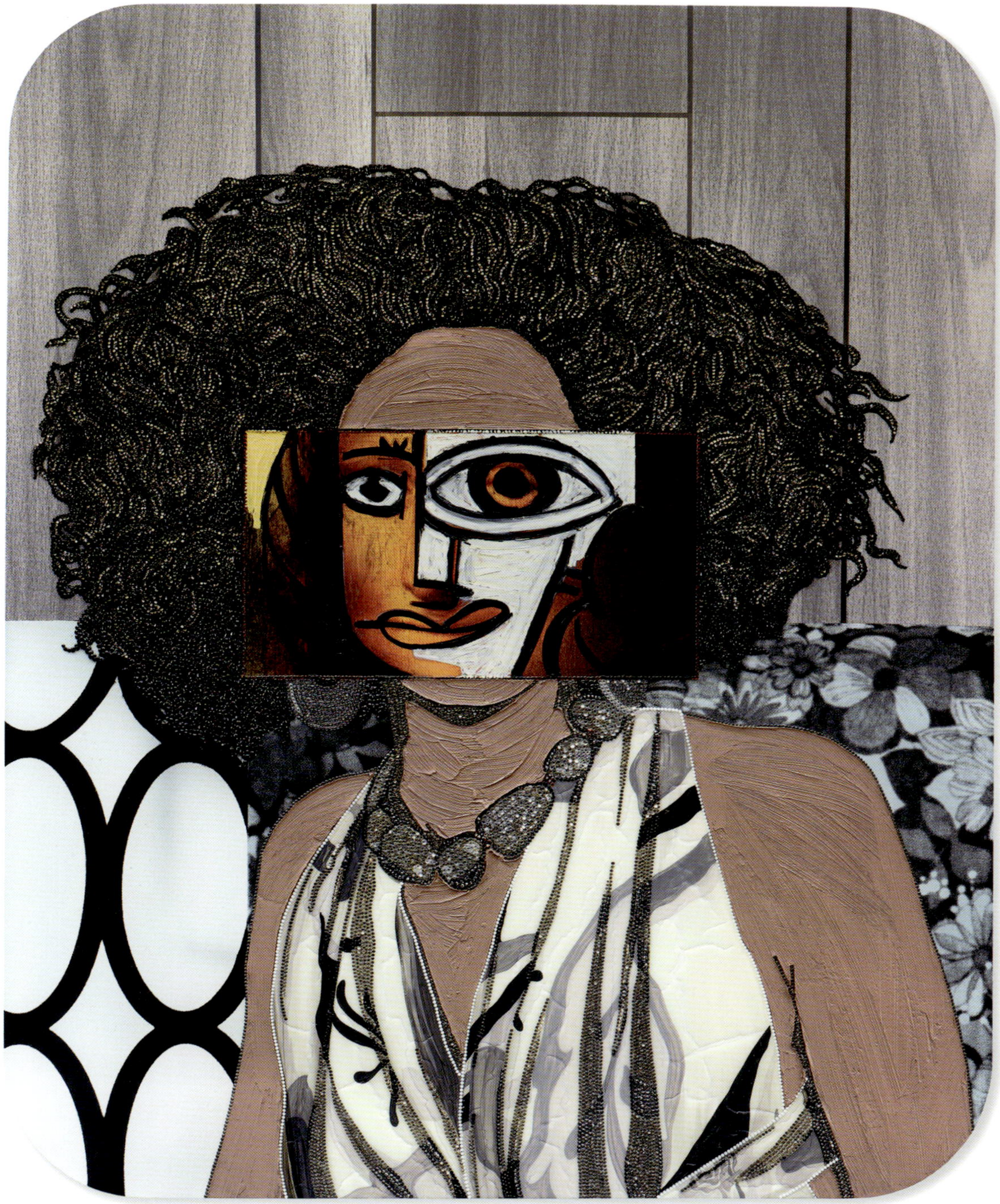

**PORTRAIT OF KALENA, 2017**

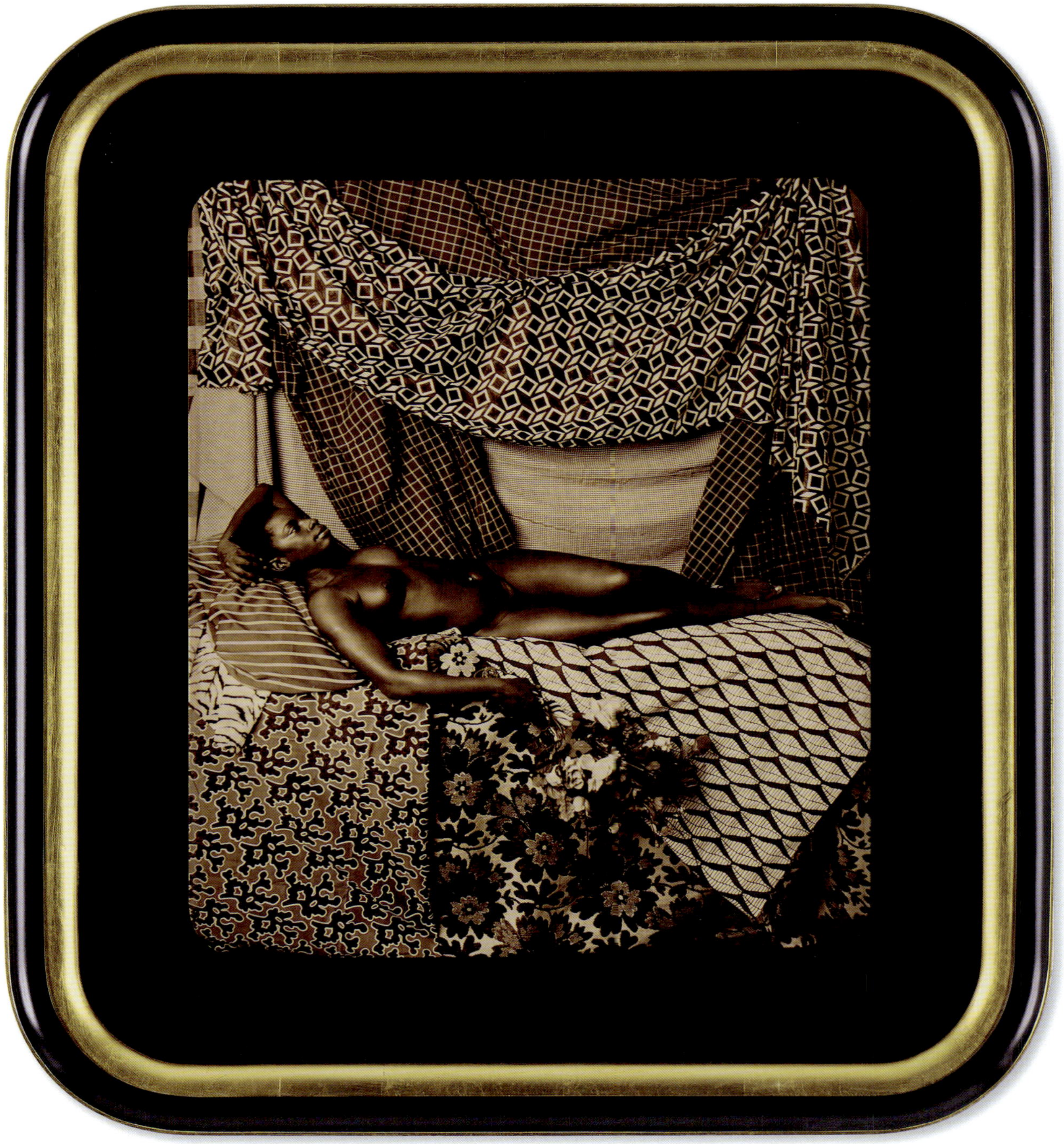



**COURBET #5 (MARIE: RELAXING), 2011**

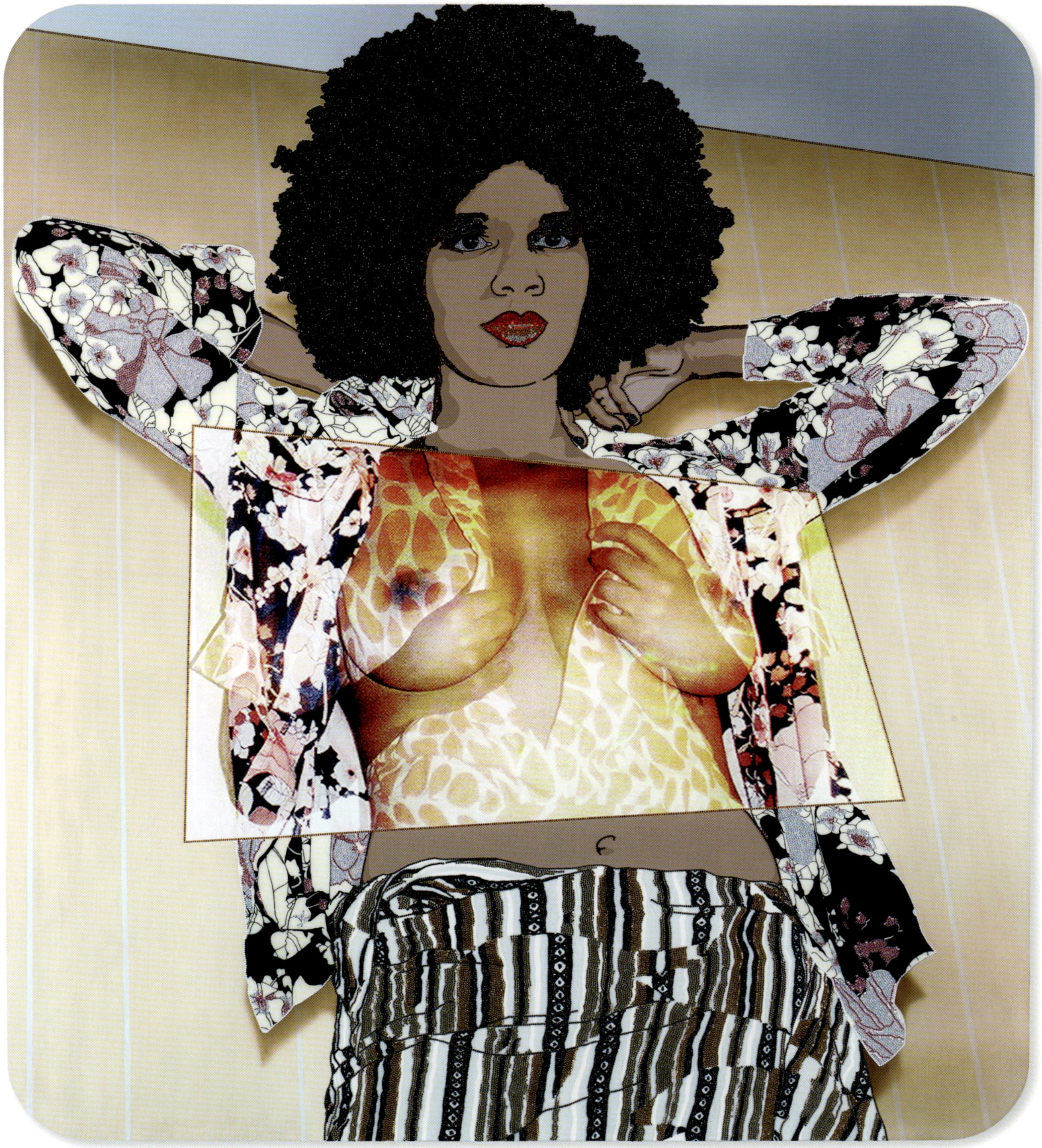

**PORTRAIT OF MAYA #10, 2017**

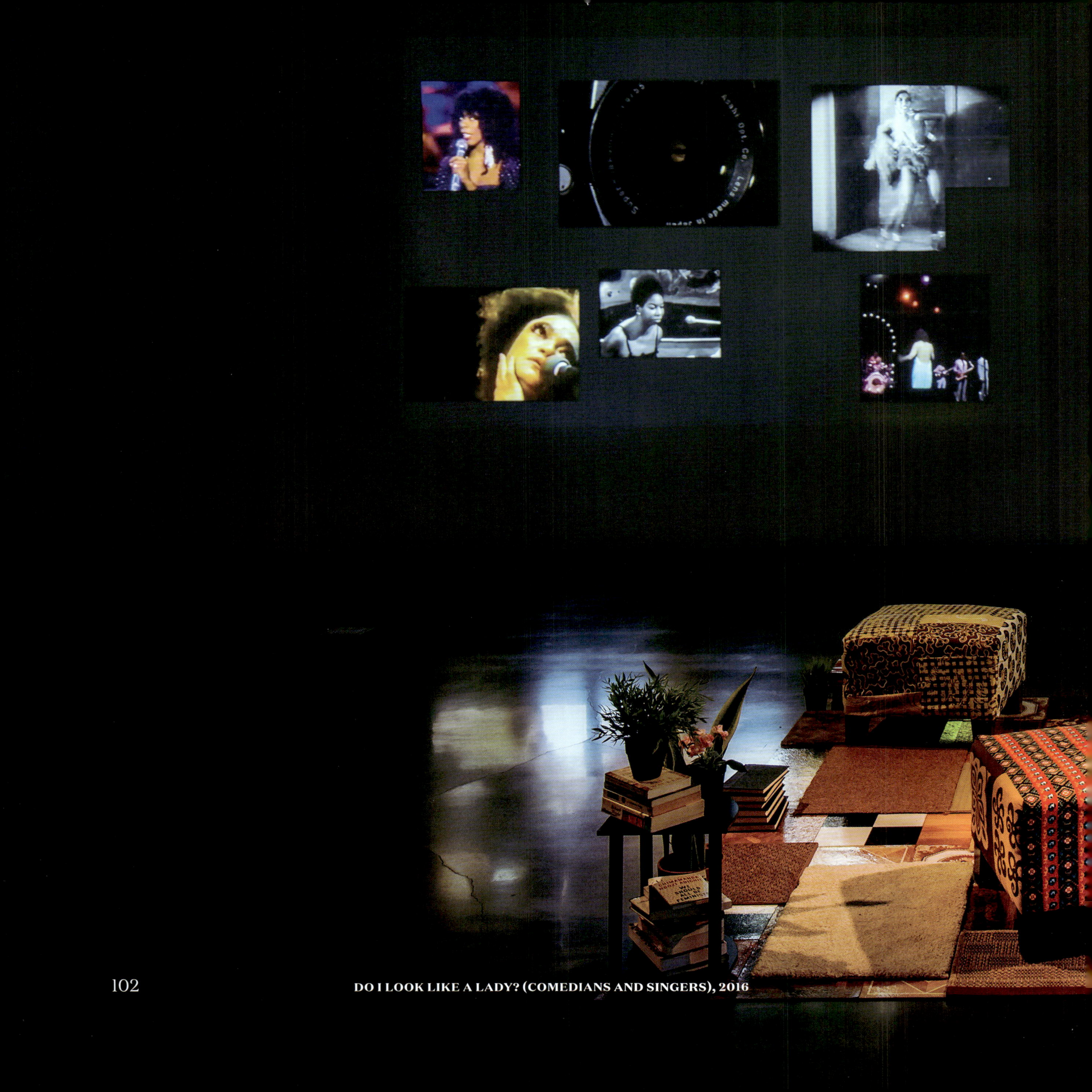

DO I LOOK LIKE A LADY? (COMEDIANS AND SINGERS), 2016

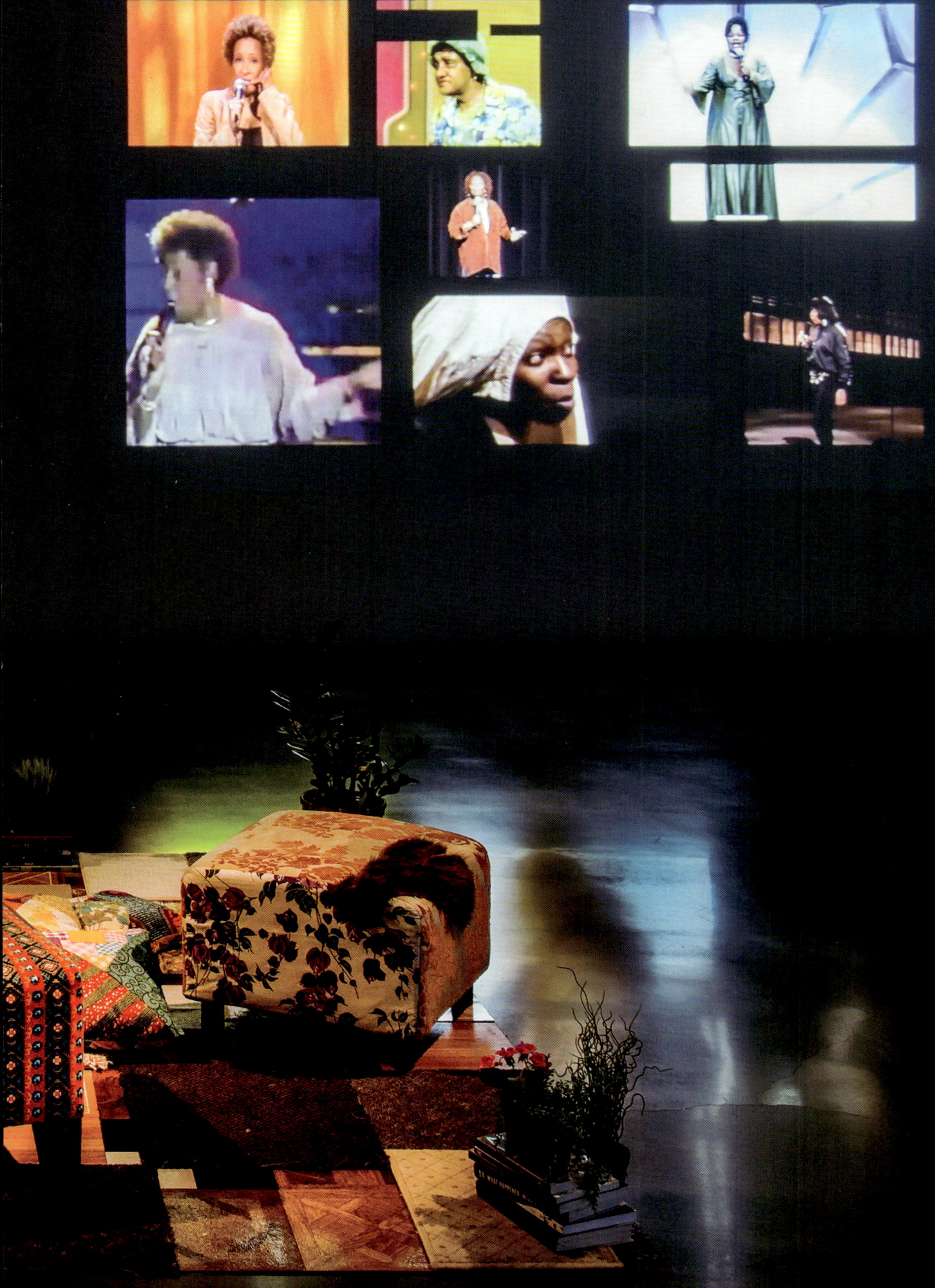

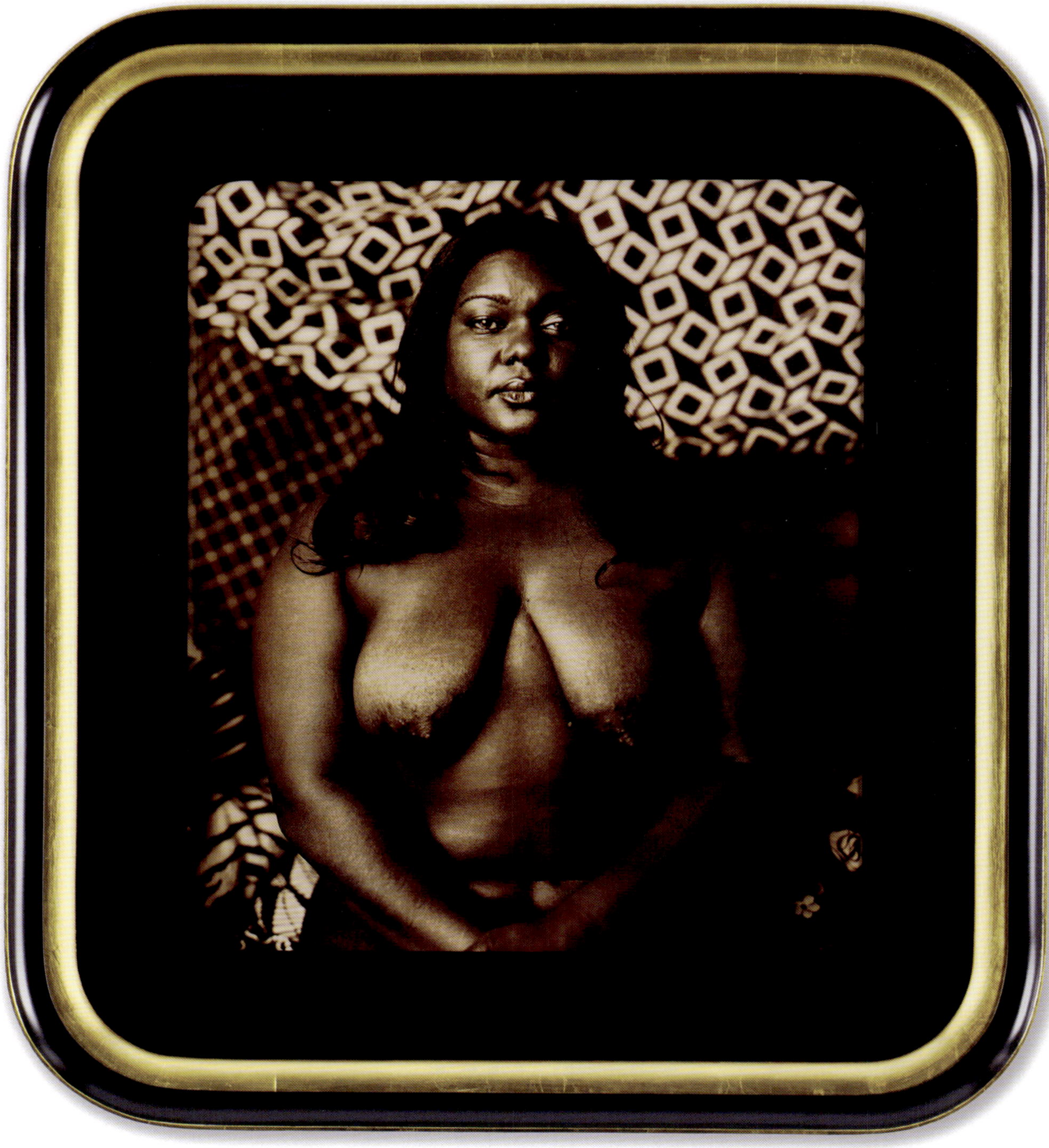



**COURBET #2 (MELODY: CENTERED), 2011**

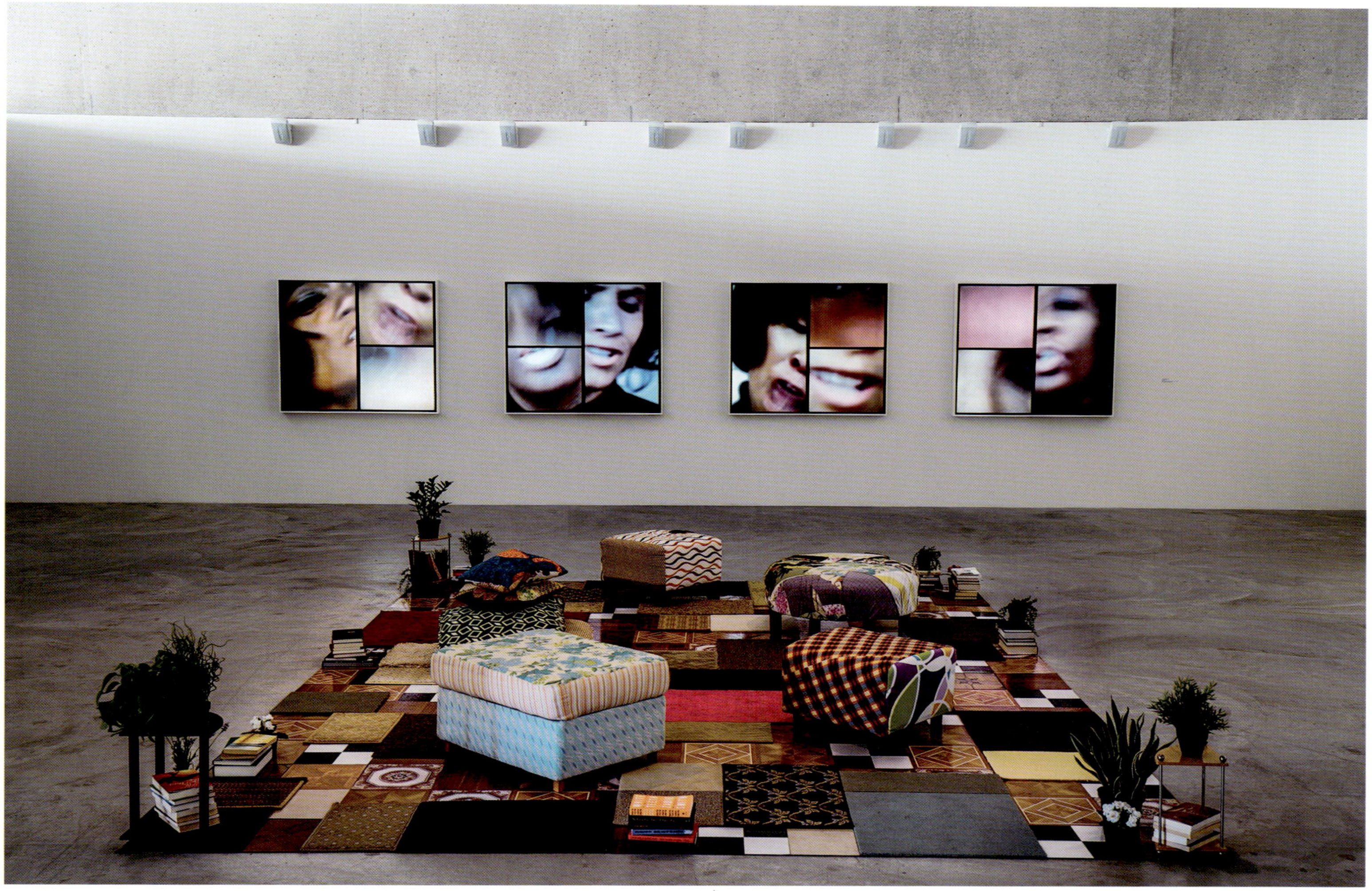

ANGELITOS NEGROS, 2016

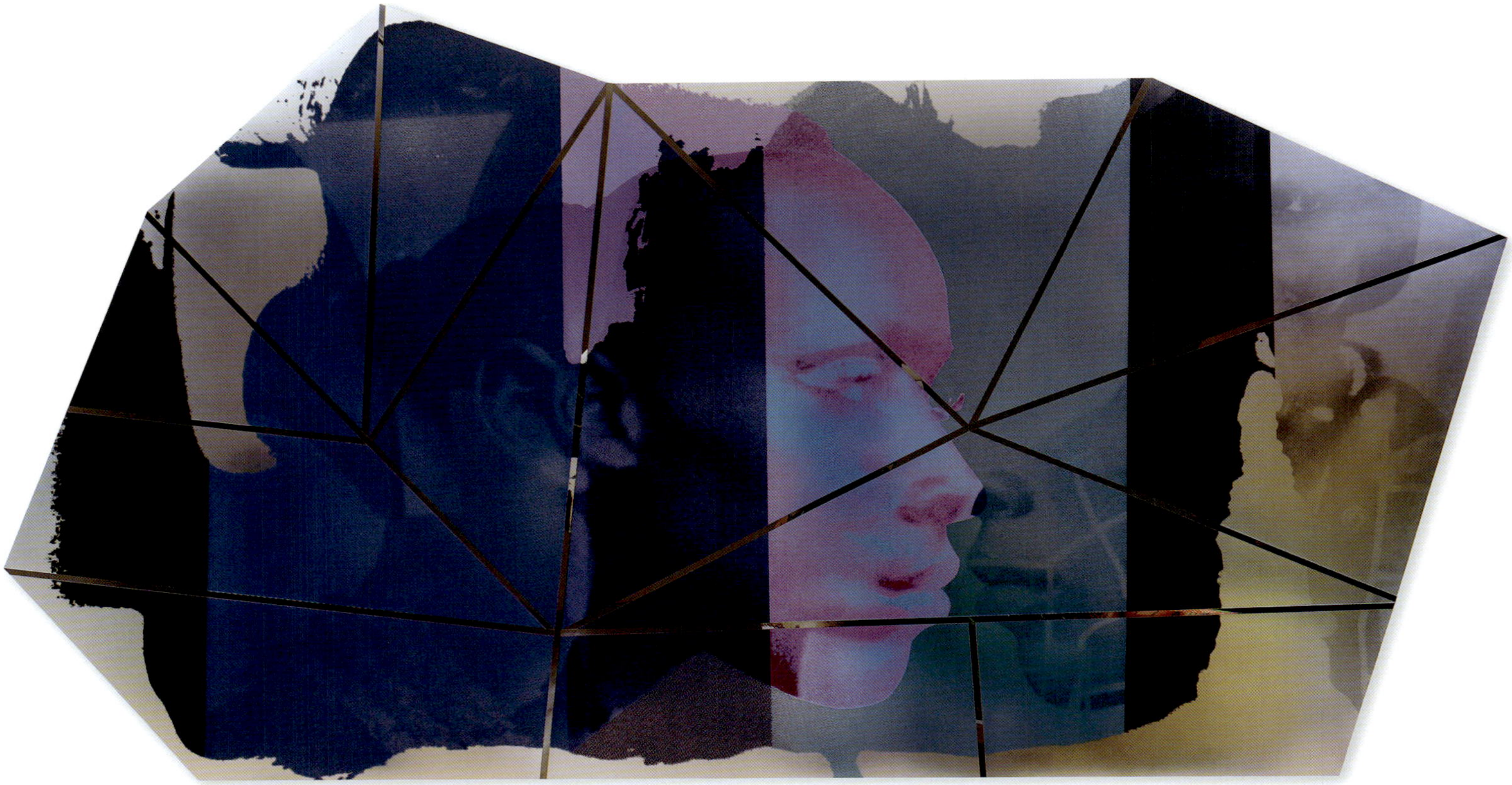



NAOMI SIMS, 2016

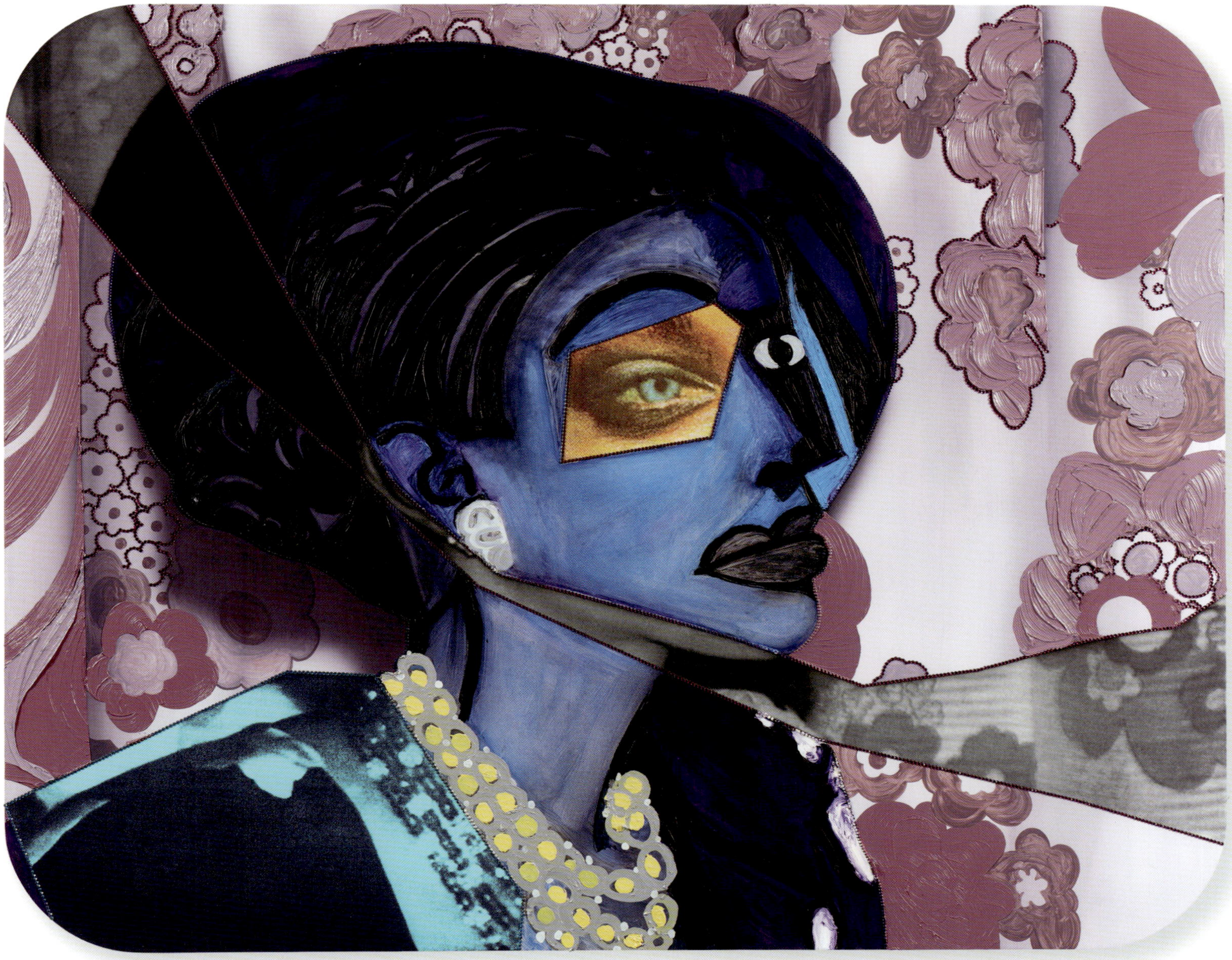

PORTRAIT OF AALIYAH, 2018

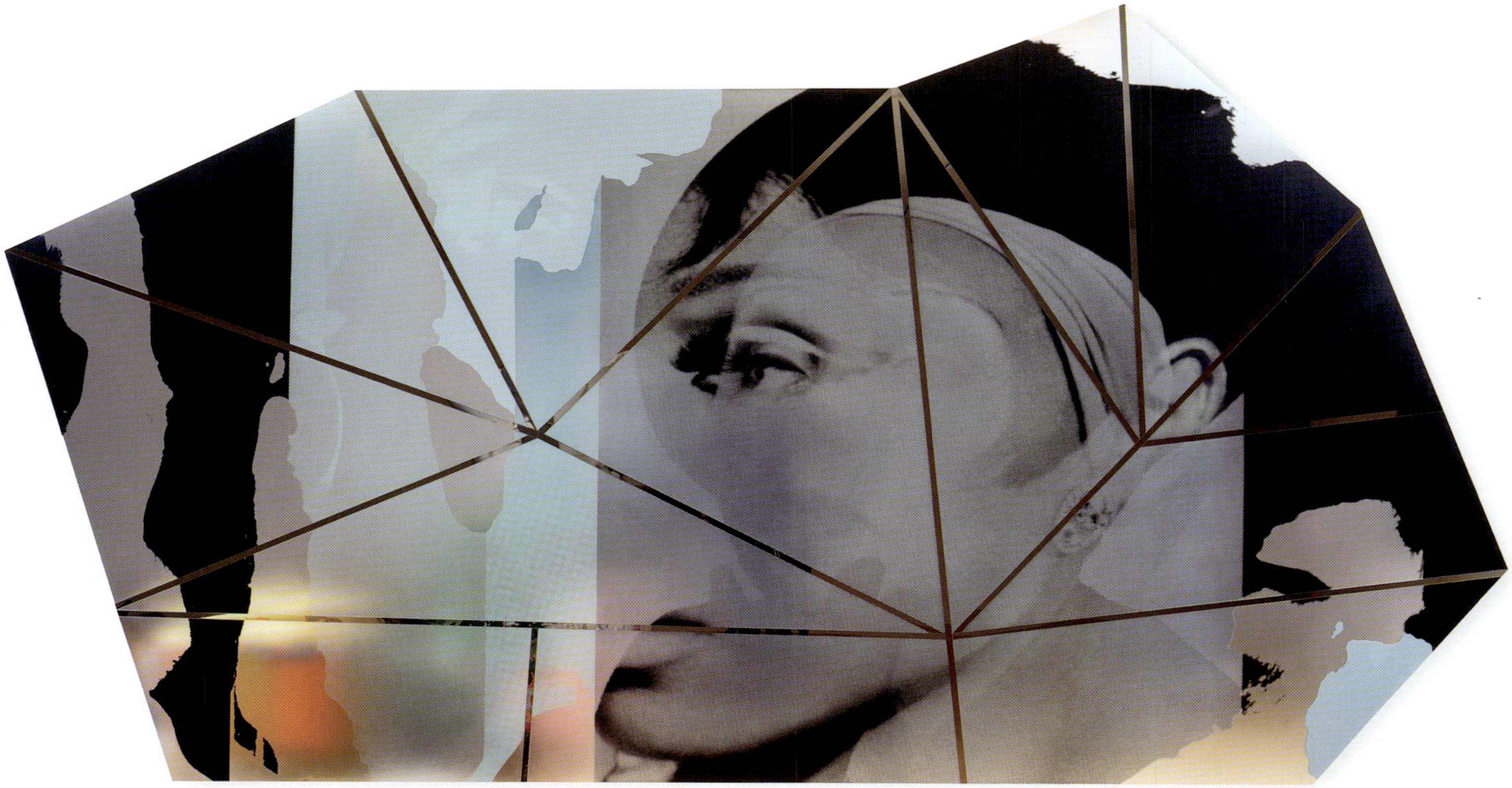



**DIAHANN CARROLL, 2016**

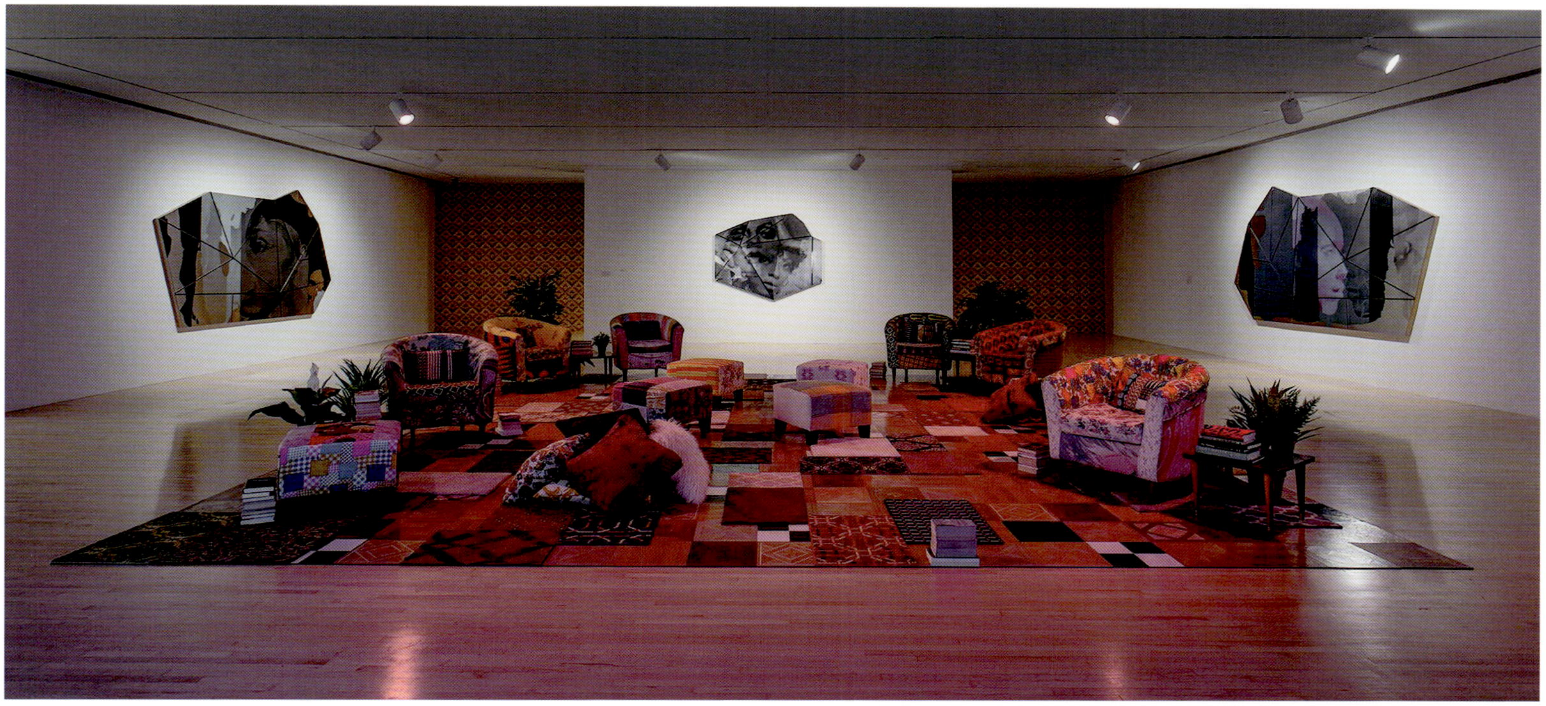

*TABLEAU FROM* **MICKALENE THOMAS: DO I LOOK LIKE A LADY?**
***AT THE MUSEUM OF CONTEMPORARY ART LA, 2016***

# *Men We Reaped* (2013)
# Jesmyn Ward

As I grew older, I became a part of my private school's community, sort of. I was a cheerleader and in the drama club, served in student government, and briefly revived the student literary magazine, but I was still *other*, racially and socioeconomically. My mother forbade me to date anyone (in or out of the school). Like most mothers in the Black South, she was terrified that I would become pregnant as a teenager. She didn't allow me to go to any of the school dances until my senior year, when I was allowed to attend my senior prom, alone. I hated all of the music. One or two of the White boys I attended school with were attracted to me, and I heard rumors that others were as well, but they wouldn't act on it because I was Black. They feared the judgment of their families and community. I found out how dangerous this intersection was when I was heavily petted by a boy one night during my senior years and the next day, in conversation with another one of my classmates, another White boy, he said: *I don't believe in the mixing of the races.* Years later, I recalled that he'd touched me, but he'd refused to kiss my mouth or my face. My otherness was physically tangible. *At least*, I thought, *my brother doesn't have to deal with this in his school.*

To cope, I spent more and more of my free time, what little there was, at school, hiding out in the library, picking random books off the shelf to read. In seventh grade I read *Gone with the Wind*; while Scarlett's and Rhett's relationship spoke to the teenage romantic in me, the defeated Confederates' vilification of the freed slaves did not. And the fact that the book and movie were so beloved in America, across regions, horrified me. *Do they really think of Black people like this?* I wondered. My time at school seemed to attest that some did. By the time I was in my junior and senior years of high school, I was reading *Roots* and *Invisible Man* and *Native Son* and *The Color Purple* and, at my father's insistence, *The Autobiography of Malcolm X*. This was the early nineties, when conscious rap groups wore African-print clothing and Chuck D exhorted us to "fight the power." I wore a Malcolm X T-shirt that my father had given me to school and I was cornered by a girl in the bathroom and told: "Well, Mimi, I see I should have worn my David Duke T-shirt today." In my reading life, I was proud of my African heritage; at school, I was reticent. While I was reading and listening to Public Enemy, I understood resistance and fighting for civil rights as strength; when I was at school, I was bewildered. At home, I'd have moments of clarity while riding down the street with one of my friends, listening to Tupac, and I'd think: *I love being Black*; then a few hours later, I'd wrestle with my hair while obsessing over my antiseptic dating and social life at school, and loathe myself. When my mother picked me up from school one day, I began telling her about a school project, and she interrupted me, speaking to the pebbly asphalt road, the corridor of trees leading us home to our trailer, and said: "Stop talking like that." As in: *Why are you speaking so properly?* As in: *Why do you sound like those White kids you go to school with, that I clean up after?* As in: *Who are you?* I shut my mouth.

—



Jesmyn Ward received her MFA from the University of Michigan and has received the MacArthur Genius Grant, a Stegner Fellowship, a John and Renee Grisham Writers Residency, and the Strauss Living Prize. She is the winner of two National Book Awards for Fiction for *Sing, Unburied, Sing* and *Salvage the Bones*.

**MICKALENE THOMAS: BIOGRAPHY**

A distinguished visual artist, filmmaker, and curator, and a 2015 United States Artists Francie Bishop Good & David Horvitz Fellow, Mickalene Thomas has exhibited extensively both nationally and internationally. She is known for paintings that combine art-historical, political, and pop-cultural references. Her work presents complex notions of femininity and challenges common definitions of beauty and aesthetic representations of women.

Thomas holds a Master of Fine Arts from Yale University and a Bachelor of Fine Arts from Pratt Institute. She has held solo museum exhibitions at the Brooklyn Museum, Santa Monica Museum of Art, Hara Museum of Contemporary Art, and L'Ecole des Beaux Arts, Monaco. Recent solo exhibitions include *Waiting on a Prime-Time Star* at Moody Center for the Arts Houston and Newcomb Art Museum New Orleans, *Mickalene Thomas: Mentors, Muses and Celebrities* at Contemporary Art Museum St. Louis, *Mickalene Thomas: Do I Look Like a Lady?* at MOCA Grand, Los Angeles, and *Muse: Mickalene Thomas Photographs* (featuring *tête-à-tête*, a Thomas-curated installation of photographs that have inspired her work) at Aperture Foundation, New York, which is scheduled to travel to several venues across the United States through 2018.

Thomas's work is in the permanent collections of many galleries and museums, including SFMoMA, Brooklyn Museum, the Guggenheim, the Whitney Museum, the Seattle Art Museum, the Smithsonian National Portrait Gallery, the Montclair Art Museum, and the Newark Museum, and was exhibited at the first International Contemporary Art Biennial, Columbia. Her work has been shown in group exhibitions at the Corcoran Gallery of Art, Washington, DC; National Portrait Gallery, Washington, DC; and Saatchi Gallery, London. Other recent group exhibitions include *Figuring History* at the Seattle Art Museum and *You Are Here* at the North Carolina Museum of Art. Her work has been featured in various catalogues and reviewed by *Artforum*, *Art in America*, the *New York Times*, the *New Yorker*, *NY Arts*, *Modern Painters*, and the *Wall Street Journal*, among others. Thomas has participated in residency programs at the Studio Museum in Harlem (2002–2003) and the Versailles Foundation Munn Artists Program in Giverny, France (2011). Recent commissions include *Better Days*, Galerie at Volkshaus, Basel, Switzerland (with Absolut Vodka Art Bureau); as well as mural projects for NY MTA, the Los Angeles County Metropolitan Transit Authority; the Art in

Embassies Program at the United States Embassy in Dakar, Senegal; and the Barclays Center, Brooklyn. Her film *Happy Birthday to a Beautiful Woman* was featured on HBO and received the Black Star Film Festival Audience Awards—Favorite Short in 2013.

Thomas has been honoured by MoMA PS1 (2015) and *Bomb* Magazine, and has received a number of accolades, including the MoCADA Artistic Advocacy Award (2015), the AICA-USA Best Show in a Commercial Space Nationally (2014), Anonymous Was A Woman Grant (2012), the Brooklyn Museum Asher B. Durand Award (2012), the Timerhi Award for Leadership in the Arts (2012), the Joan Mitchell Grant (2009), and the Rema Hort Mann Grant (2007).

Mickalene Thomas is represented by Lehmann Maupin, New York and Hong Kong; Kavi Gupta Gallery, Chicago and Berlin; Susanne Vielmetter Los Angeles Projects; and Galerie Nathalie Obadia, Paris and Brussels. She lives and works in New York.

**LIST OF WORKS**

*Angelitos Negros,* 2016
Video (four channels, colour, sound, 23 mins 9 secs)
124.5 × 142.2 × 8.9 cm
Edition 1 of 3, with 2 AP
Courtesy of the artist
**PAGE 105**

—

*Blues,* 2016
Silkscreen ink and acrylic on mirrored acrylic mounted on wood panel
182.9 × 152.4 cm
Courtesy of the artist and Lehmann Maupin, New York, Hong Kong, and Seoul
**PAGE 45**

—

*Courbet #2 (Melody: Centered),* 2011
Polaroid
61 × 50.8 cm (unframed)
88.3 × 79.4 cm (framed)
Courtesy of the artist and Lehmann Maupin, New York, Hong Kong, and Seoul
**PAGE 104**

—

*Courbet #4 (Marie: Centered),* 2011
Polaroid
61 × 50.8 cm (unframed)
88.3 × 79.4 cm (framed)
Courtesy of the artist and Lehmann Maupin, New York, Hong Kong, and Seoul
**PAGE 61**

*Courbet #5 (Marie: Relaxing),* 2011
Polaroid
61 × 50.8 cm (unframed)
88.3 × 79.4 cm (framed)
Private collection, Monaco
**PAGE 100**

—

*Diahann Carroll,* 2016
Silkscreen ink on acrylic mirror mounted on wood panel
182.9 × 340.4 cm
Courtesy of the artist and Lehmann Maupin, New York, Hong Kong, and Seoul
**PAGE 108**

—

*Diahann Carroll #2,* 2017
Silkscreen ink on acrylic mirror mounted on wood panel
182.9 × 152.4 × 5.1 cm
Courtesy of the artist and Galerie Nathalie Obadia, Paris/Brussels
**COVER (DETAIL); PAGE 98**

—

*Diana Ross,* 2016
Silkscreen ink on acrylic mirror mounted on wood panel
182.9 × 152.4 cm
Collection of Michael L. & Roberta S. Joseph
**PAGE 120**

—

*Do I Look Like a Lady? (Comedians and Singers),* 2016
Video (two-channel projection, colour, sound, 12 mins 34 secs)
Edition 2 of 3, with 2 AP
Courtesy of the artist
**PAGES 102–103**

—

*I Learned the Hard Way,* 2010
Rhinestones, acrylic, and enamel on wood panel
304.8 × 243.8 cm
Collection of the Montreal Museum of Fine Arts
**PAGE 75**

—

*je t'aime deux,* 2014
Film (four-channel installation; 20 mins. 1 sec.)
Edition 1 of 5, with 2 APs
Courtesy of the artist
**PAGES 62–63**

—

*Le déjeuner sur l'herbe: Les trois femmes noires,* 2010
Rhinestones, acrylic, and enamel on wood panel
304.8 × 731.5 cm
The Rachel and Jean-Pierre Lehmann Collection
**PAGES 50–51**

—

*Living Room Tableau 1,* 2018
Ottomans, chairs, carpet tiles, cushions, plants, and various accessories
Variable dimensions
Courtesy of the artist

—

*Living Room Tableau 2,* 2018
Ottomans, chairs, carpet tiles, cushions, plants, and various accessories
Variable dimensions
Courtesy of the artist

—

*Love's Been Good to Me #3,* 2010
Rhinestones, acrylic, and enamel on wood panel
243.8 × 182.9 cm
Private collection, Toronto
**PAGE 83**

—

*Me as Muse,* 2016
Multimedia video installation (4 mins. 2 secs.)
146.1 × 269.9 × 81.3 cm
AP1, edition of 3, with 2 APs
Courtesy of the artist
**PAGE 4**

—

*Ms. Celie's Blues,* 2016
Silkscreen ink and acrylic on mirrored acrylic mounted on wood panel
182.9 × 558.8 cm
Courtesy of the artist and Lehmann Maupin, New York, Hong Kong, and Seoul
**PAGES 48–49**

—

*Naomi Sims,* 2016
Silkscreen ink on acrylic mirror mounted on wood
182.9 × 340.4 cm
Courtesy of the artist and Lehmann Maupin, New York, Hong Kong, and Seoul
**PAGE 106**

—

*Naomi Sims #2,* 2016
Silkscreen ink on acrylic mirror mounted on wood
152.4 × 182.9 cm
Courtesy of the artist and Lehmann Maupin, New York, Hong Kong, and Seoul
**PAGE 44**

—

*Portrait of Aaliyah,* 2018
Rhinestones, oil stick, acrylic, and oil paint on wood panel
121.9 × 152.4 cm
The Aaron Pietrykowski Collection
**PAGE 107**

—

*Portrait of Kalena,* 2017
Rhinestones, oil stick, acrylic, and oil paint on wood panel
152.4 × 121.9 cm
Collection of Ms. Ursula M. Burns
**PAGE 99**

—

*Portrait of Marie,* 2015
Rhinestones, acrylic, and oil on wood panel
121.9 × 91.4 cm
Harry David Collection
**PAGE 29**

—

*Portrait of Maya #10,* 2017
Rhinestones and acrylic on canvas mounted on wood panel
243.8 × 213.4 cm
Private collection, Toronto
**PAGE 101**

—

*Qusuquzah, une très belle négresse #3,* 2012
Rhinestones, acrylic, and oil on wood panel
228.6 × 203.2 cm
Collection of the National Gallery of Canada
**PAGE 53**

—

*Shinique: Now I Know,* 2015
Rhinestones, acrylic, and oil on wood panel
243.8 × 304.8 cm
Courtesy of Mary Boone Gallery, New York
**PAGE 41**

—

*Shug Kisses Celie,* 2016
Silkscreen ink and acrylic on mirrored acrylic mounted on wood panel
182.9 × 152.4 cm
Westmoreland Museum of American Art
**PAGE 46**

—

*Sister: Shug Avery Breakfast,* 2016
Silkscreen ink and acrylic on mirrored acrylic mounted on wood panel
182.9 × 152.4 cm
Courtesy of the artist and Lehmann Maupin, New York, Hong Kong, and Seoul
**PAGE 47**

—



## PHOTO CREDITS

Page 19: Photo by Benoît Touchard/Mathieu Rabeau. Image © Musée d'Orsay/RMN-Grand Palais/Art Resource, NY.

Page 20: Mickalene Thomas, *Le déjeuner sur l'herbe: Les trois femmes noires*, 2010. Chromogenic print, 121.9 × 152.4 cm. Edition 3 of 5, with 2 APs. Courtesy of the artist.

Page 21: Photo © The Museum of Modern Art/Licensed by SCALA/Art Resource, NY.

Page 111: Tableau from *Mickalene Thomas: Do I Look Like a Lady?* at the Museum of Contemporary Art LA, 2016. 609.6 × 609.6 cm. Photo courtesy of MoCA LA.

## SELECTED BIBLIOGRAPHY

Adichie, Chimamanda Ngozi. *Americanah*. Toronto: Penguin Random House Canada, 2013.

Danticat, Edwidge. "We Are Ugly, But We Are Here." In *Women Writing Resistance: Essays on Latin America and the Caribbean*, edited by Jennifer Browdy, 23–27. Cambridge: South End Press, 2005.

O'Grady, Lorraine. "Olympia's Maid: Reclaiming Black Female Subjectivity." In *The Feminism and Visual Culture Reader*, 2nd edition, edited by Amelia Jones, 208–220. New York: Routledge, 2010.

Silvera, Makeda. "Man Royals and Sodomites: Some Thoughts on the Invisibility of Afro-Caribbean Lesbians." In *Piece of My Heart: A Lesbian of Colour Anthology*, edited by Makeda Silvera, 14–26. Toronto: Sister Vision Press, 1991.

Walker, Alice. *The Color Purple*. New York: Harcourt, 1982.

Ward, Jesmyn. *Men We Reaped*. New York: Bloomsbury USA, 2013.

Published in 2018 by the Art Gallery of Ontario and Goose Lane Editions. 

The Art Gallery of Ontario is partially funded by the Ontario Ministry of Culture. Additional operating support is received from the City of Toronto, the Department of Canadian Heritage, and the Canada Council for the Arts.

Contemporary programming at the Art Gallery of Ontario is supported by

Canada Council for the Arts Conseil des arts du Canada

Goose Lane Editions acknowledges the generous support of the Government of Canada, the Canada Council for the Arts, and the Government of New Brunswick.

Printed and bound in Canada

10 9 8 7 6 5 4 3 2 1

Library and Archives Canada Cataloguing in Publication

Mickalene Thomas : femmes noires/edited by Andrea Andersson & Julie Crooks.

Catalogue of an exhibition held at the Art Gallery of Ontario from November 29, 2018 to March 24, 2019. Includes bibliographical references. Copublished by Goose Lane Editions. ISBN 978-1-988788-08-1 (hardcover : Art Gallery of Ontario).— ISBN 978-1-77310-123-1 (hardcover : Goose Lane Editions)

1. Thomas, Mickalene, 1971- — Exhibitions. 2. Exhibition catalogs. I. Andersson, Andrea, editor II. Crooks, Julie, 1962-, editor III. Art Gallery of Ontario, issuing body, host institution IV. Thomas, Mickalene, 1971- . Works. Selections. V. Title: Femmes noires.

N6537.T45A4 2018
709.2
C2018-905221-X

Published in conjunction with the exhibition *Mickalene Thomas: Femmes Noires*

Art Gallery of Ontario
Toronto, Ontario, Canada
November 29, 2018
–March 24, 2019

Contemporary Arts Center, New Orleans
November 2019–March 2020

*Mickalene Thomas: Femmes Noires* is organized by the Art Gallery of Ontario and the Contemporary Arts Center, New Orleans.

Art Gallery of Ontario
317 Dundas Street West
Toronto, Ontario M5T 1G4
Canada
www.ago.ca

Goose Lane Editions
500 Beaverbrook Court,
Suite 330
Fredericton, New Brunswick
E3B 5X4
Canada
www.gooselane.com

**ART GALLERY OF ONTARIO**

**Lead Sponsor**
CIBC

**Lead Supporters**
Maxine Granovsky Gluskin & Ira Gluskin
Liza Mauer & Andrew Sheiner

**Generously supported by**
Partners in Art
The Schulich Foundation

**CONTEMPORARY ARTS CENTER**

**Presenting Sponsor**
The Helis Foundation

**PUBLICATION**

**Edited by**
Andrea Andersson
Julie Crooks

**Managing Editor**
Jim Shedden

**Production and Copy Editors**
Sarah Liss
Alicia Peres

**Publishing Coordinator**
Robyn Lew

**Proofreader**
Judy Phillips

**Designer**
Lauren Wickware

**Pre-Press and Printing**
Type A Print Inc.

**AGO EXHIBITION**

**Curator**
Julie Crooks

**Chief Curator**
Julian Cox

**Project Manager**
Valentine Moreno

**Interpretive Planner**
Shiralee Hudson Hill

**Curatorial Administrative Assistant**
Jill Offenbeck

**Editor**
Sarah Liss

**Design and Graphics**
Malene Hjørngaard
Evelina Petrauskas
Evelyn Quinn
Flavio Trevisan

**EXHIBITIONS AND COLLECTIONS**

**Chief, Exhibitions and Collections**
Christy Thompson

**Director of Exhibitions**
Jessica Bright

**Registration**
Donna Austria
Cindy Brouse
Jerry Drozdowsky
Tim Hardacre
Joel Herman
Dale Mahar
Curtis Strilchuk

**Collection Information**
Eva Athanasiu
Tracy Mallon-Jensen
Liana Radvak
Olga Zotova

**Conservators**
Meaghan Monaghan
Sherry Phillips
Maria Sullivan
Sjoukje Van der Laan
Katharine Whitman

**Logistics and Art Services**
Curtis Amisich
Michael Beynon
Andrew Bugden
Scott Cameron
Corinne Carlson
Marco Cheuk
Patric Colosimo
Brian Davis
Mark Dudiak
Randal Fedje
Tina Giovinazzo
Eric Glavin
Brian Groombridge
Roland Hardy
Iain Hoadley
Matthew Janisse
Ruth Jones
Charles Kettle
David Kinsman
Jason Laudadio
Alison Lindsay
Paul Mathiesen
Doug Moore
Ben Oakley
Hagop Ohannessian
Jacques Oule
Angelo Pedari
Sabine Schaefer
Carmen Schroeder
Damian Seguin
Harry Singh
Jelena Sisko
David Stasyna
Craig Whiteside
Darin Yorston
Tanya Zhilinsky

**PUBLIC PROGRAMMING AND LEARNING**

**Acting Head, Public Programming & Learning**
Keri Ryan

**Director, Public Programs**
Devyani Saltzman

**Public Programming**
Kathleen McLean
Bojana Stancic

**Media Production**
Matthew Scott
Danny Winchester

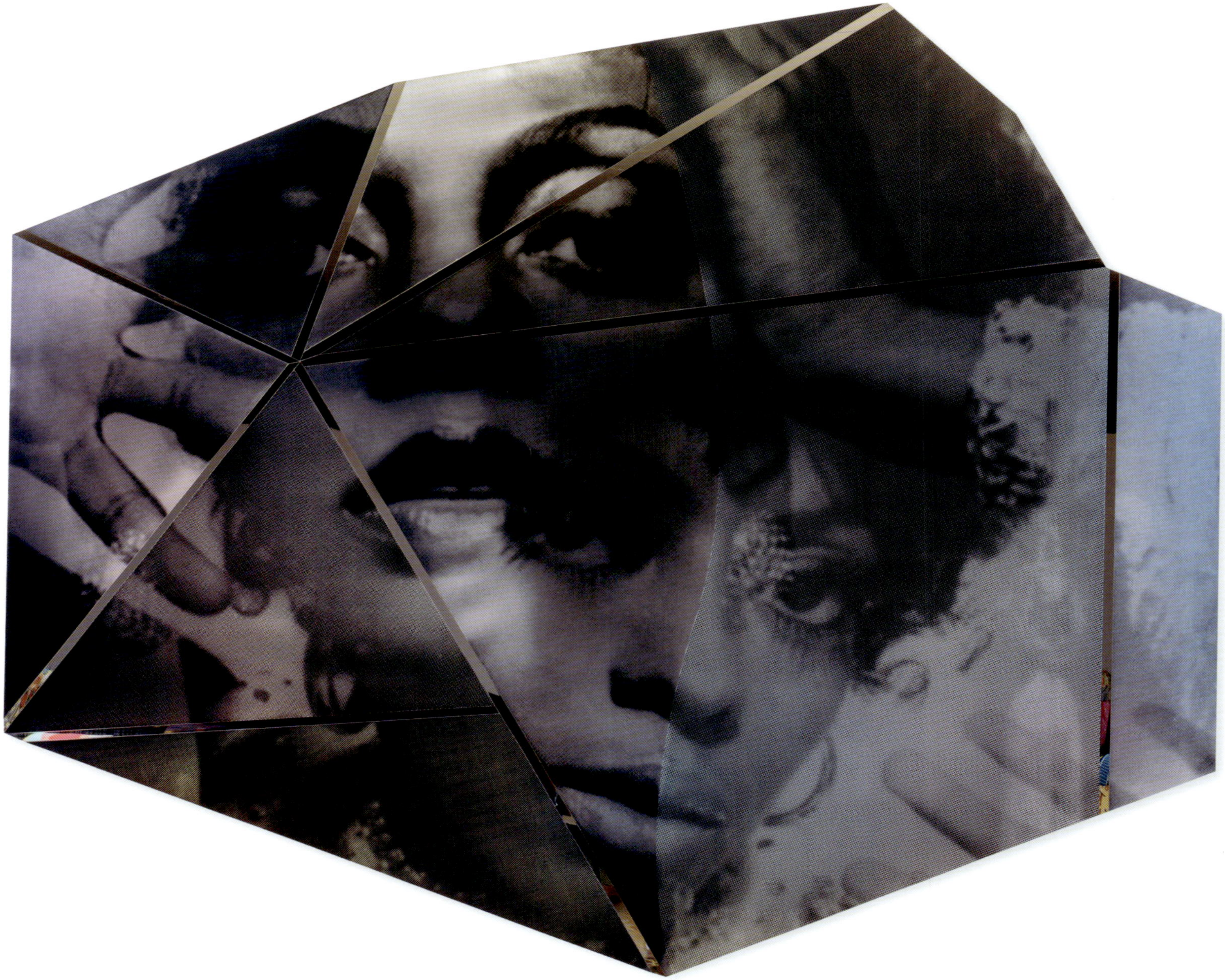

DIANA ROSS, 2016